The People's Bible Teachings

MAN

From Glory to Ashes and Back

Lyle L. Luchterhand

NORTHWESTERN PUBLISHING HOUSE
Milwaukee, Wisconsin

All Scripture quotations, unless otherwise indicated, are taken from the HOLY BIBLE, NEW INTERNATIONAL VERSION®. NIV®. Copyright © 1973, 1978, 1984 by International Bible Society. Used by permission of Zondervan Publishing House. All rights reserved.

The "NIV" and "New International Version" trademarks are registered in the United States Patent and Trademark Office by International Bible Society. Use of either trademark requires the permission of International Bible Society.

All rights reserved. No part of this publication may be reproduced, stored in a retrieval system, or transmitted in any form or by any means—electronic, mechanical, photocopy, recording, or otherwise—except for brief quotations in reviews, without prior permission from the publisher.

Library of Congress Card 97-069964
Northwestern Publishing House
1250 N. 113th St., Milwaukee, WI 53226-3284
© 1998 by Northwestern Publishing House.
Published 1998
Printed in the United States of America
ISBN 0-8100-0799-1

Table of Contents

Editor's Preface

The People's Bible Teachings is a series of books on all of the main doctrinal teachings of the Bible.

Following the pattern set by The People's Bible series, these books are written especially for laypeople. Theological terms, when used, are explained in everyday language so that people can understand them. The authors show how Christian doctrine is drawn directly from clear passages of Scripture and then how those doctrines apply to people's faith and life. Most importantly, these books show how every teaching of Scripture points to Christ, our only Savior.

The authors of The People's Bible Teachings are parish pastors and professors who have had years of experience teaching the Bible. They are men of scholarship and practical insight.

We take this opportunity to express our gratitude to Professor Leroy Dobberstein of Wisconsin Lutheran Seminary, Mequon, Wisconsin, and Professor Thomas Nass of Martin Luther College, New Ulm, Minnesota, for serving as consultants for this series. Their insights and assistance have been invaluable.

We pray that the Lord will use these volumes to help his people grow in their faith, knowledge, and understanding of his saving teachings, which he has revealed to us in the Bible. To God alone be the glory.

Curtis A. Jahn
Series Editor

Introduction

On a clear night, lift your eyes to the heavens. How many stars do you see? Astronomers say there are some six thousand stars visible to the naked eye. Look into a telescope, and you can see even more.

Those who make the sky their lifestudy estimate that there may be over one hundred billion stars in our Milky Way galaxy alone. Astronomers also estimate that there may be one hundred billion galaxies. Some stars are thought to be 16 billion light-years from the earth. One light-year is a distance of 5.88 trillion miles! The size of some stars also boggles the mind. One giant star, called Betelgeuse (pronounced like *beetle juice*), has a diameter several hundred times that of the sun.

How small is Earth when compared to the great masses and vast distances of the other bodies in the universe! Smaller still is the sum of humanity that inhabits Earth. Poor, helpless man* . . . helpless before natural catastrophes like earthquakes and floods . . . helpless before the winds and the tides.

The psalmist asked God, "What is man that you are mindful of him?" (Psalm 8:4). The question begs for an answer. What is man that the powerful God who created this marvelous universe would pay any attention to him? And why would God want to sacrifice his only Son on a cross to take away man's sins?

---

*Throughout this book the author uses the term *man* and the masculine pronouns to refer to the human race and to human nature in the interest of simplicity and brevity and in accordance with time-honored usage. No demeaning of the female sex is intended.

Yes, what is man? What is man's origin? What is his worth? What are his capabilities? What is his destiny? At one extreme, the disciples of New Age philosophy believe that man is God. At the other extreme, evolutionists teach that man is only a highly developed animal and the product of chance. But the Bible tells us that man is neither God nor animal. Man is God's special creature whom he dearly loves and watches over.

What is man? That is the question we will address in this book. We are convinced that the correct answer to this question can be learned only from God. Only our Creator knows our true worth and capabilities. Only our Creator knows the truth about our origin and destiny. He knows us much better than we know ourselves.

In the following pages, we intend to let God himself tell the story of man as he reveals it in the Bible. It is a fascinating account. It is a story that follows man from glory to ashes and back.

Part I

Glory

1

The Glorious Purpose of Man

What is the purpose of our lives? Why are we here? In our hectic society, many of us rush back and forth, chasing from one urgent task to another. The things that often fill our lives and our mindless haste in doing them may betray the fact that our lives have no real direction. We may even be going in the wrong direction! But overwhelmed by the crush of everyday duties and obligations, we find little time to consider such a profound subject as the reason for our existence. It would seem such a matter is better left to theologians and philosophers.

Yet everyone sets personal goals. Everyone has reasons for living. This may not always be evident in what we say, but it is evident in how we live. For some people the purpose of life is accumulating wealth, acquiring knowledge, or pursuing respect from their peers. Others live unselfishly for family and friends. Still others simply live to have a good time.

God's purpose for us

But what is the purpose God has in mind for us? The Bible says God created us for his glory (Isaiah 43:7). He created us and placed us on Earth to serve him and glorify his name. That is why the apostle Paul wrote, "Whatever you do, do it all for the glory of God" (1 Corinthians 10:31). From the moment we rub the sleep from our eyes one morning to the moment we wake up the next morning, God wants everything we do to glorify him. Jesus told his disciples, "Let your light shine before men" (Matthew 5:16). Why? Not that *they* might be praised, but that others might see their good deeds and praise *their Father in heaven* (verse 16). Similarly, Peter encouraged his readers to declare the praises of him who called them out of darkness into his wonderful light (1 Peter 2:9). The Bible repeatedly tells us that God wants us to glorify him, to give him honor, to show everyone what a wonderful, kind, loving, and generous God he is.

Everything created for God's glory

It shouldn't surprise us that God created us for his glory. The Bible tells us that this is the purpose for all creation. Consider Paul's words to the Romans: "From him [God] and through him and to him are all things. To him be the glory forever!" (Romans 11:36). "*From* him . . . are all things" reminds us that God is the source of everything. Only because of him do we have life and existence. "*Through* him . . . are all things" reminds us that we prosper only by his blessing. Every good thing comes through him. "*To* him are all things" reveals the ultimate purpose of all creation: to give praise and glory to God.

The angels are repeatedly urged by God to praise him (Psalm 103:20,21; 148:2), which shows the purpose for which these powerful and magnificent creatures were created. Even inanimate things glorify God. In Psalm 148 the sun, moon, and stars, the mountains, and even lightning and hail are called upon to praise him. And lest we think that the things God created without breath and vocal cords cannot accomplish their task of praising God, God tells us that the heavens declare his glory (Psalm 19:1).

Everything God made testifies to his power, wisdom, and goodness. The sun, the moon, the oceans, even the frogs—all glorify God by being what he intended them to be.

Only man rebels

Of all God's creation, only sinful man rebels at the thought of glorifying the Creator. Think of our own poor attitudes toward public worship. We would hasten to say we don't hate God; we just don't always have time for him! We are preoccupied with our work, our families, our recreation, and the various responsibilities of life. But according to God's point of view, we *do* hate him according to our sinful nature (Romans 8:7). Lack of love is hatred, as far as God is concerned (Matthew 12:30).

Every day God pours his blessings upon people who choose to ignore him. Every day he gives us air to breathe and water to drink. He gives us jobs, families, time, and money. And what do we do? We use God's generosity against him! Our preoccupation with God's blessings becomes the reason we have no time or money for him!

People who have no time for God are like a spoiled little boy who has a birthday party. He invites all kinds
of people to his party. But he really doesn't care who
comes, how long they stay, or whether they have a good
time. He only cares about their gifts. In fact, he wouldn't
mind if they would just drop off their gifts at the door
and leave. He wants the gifts, but he doesn't want the
people who bring them. Similarly, many people want all
the gifts God can give them, but they want nothing to do
with him.

God loves his world

It was not God's intention to give his gifts and then
walk away. God did not place a plastic bubble around creation, which he vowed never to penetrate. He has not
imposed on himself an exile from the world he made.
From the very beginning, God did not want man to experience a life without him. Instead, God demonstrated
that he wanted man to have a loving, personal relationship with his Creator.

The book of Genesis suggests that God communicated
with man regularly in the Garden of Eden. God walked
and talked with Adam and Eve. The Bible is filled with
instances in which God lovingly interfered in his world to
care for his human creatures. For example, God saved
Noah from the flood (Genesis 6–8), rescued the Israelites
from slavery in Egypt (Exodus 1–14), and fed Elijah at the
brook Kerith (1 Kings 17:1-6). God did not create this
world and then walk away and ignore it.

In thankful response to God's eternal love and watch-
ful care, man is expected to serve God. Man is not
to center his life on himself or the world. He is to center

his life on God. Indeed, his whole purpose in life is to glorify God.

Is God selfish?

Some people object to the idea that God created everything for his own glory. They claim this is unworthy of God, because it makes him proud and selfish. The church has always answered this objection, first of all, by saying it is *unscriptural.* The Bible plainly says God created us for his glory (Isaiah 43:7) and that "the LORD works out everything for his own ends" (Proverbs 16:4). Second, the objection is *unreasonable* because it judges God by human standards. Third, the objection is *humanistic* because it attempts to put man in God's place. If the world were not made for God's glory, then it must have been made for man's. Then man becomes the end goal of all creation and the focal point of all history! God is forced to kneel at man's feet.

What nobler or more acceptable purpose could man have than to glorify God? In Job 38 God reminds Job that he laid the earth's foundation (verse 4), shut up the sea behind doors (verse 8), walked in the recesses of the deep (verse 16), and sent the lightning bolts on their way (verse 35). In chapter 39 God says he knows when the mountain goats give birth (verse 1), gives the ostrich swiftness (verse 18), gives the horse strength (verse 19), and makes the eagle soar at his command (verse 27). Two more chapters of Job list the mighty works of God. Our works are nothing compared to his. Why would we rebel at giving God the praise that is due him? Even worse, why would we try to steal that praise for ourselves?

The greatest thing God did for us was to carry out his plan of salvation, at which even the angels marvel (1 Peter 1:12). But *why* did God send his Son to die an agonizing death on a cross? David gives us the answer in the familiar words of Psalm 23: "He restores my soul. He guides me in paths of righteousness *for his name's sake*" (verse 3). He saves us for his name's sake! God has a reputation for goodness among his saints, a reputation he maintains by saving us. Thus God intends to be glorified through our salvation.

At the same time, God's plan of salvation cannot be considered selfish, because God carried out his plan for us. Because Jesus died, we live. Because Jesus was forsaken by God, we are embraced and welcomed by God into heaven. God's plan of salvation is anything but selfish!

Living God's purpose

God's purpose for every one of us is that we might glorify him. In fact, sometimes God may have in mind a very specific way in which we can glorify him. The story of Esther illustrates this. Esther was the wife of the vain and temperamental King Xerxes of Persia. Under the influence of a very persuasive government official named Haman, Xerxes decreed that on a certain day every Jew in the Persian empire was to be killed. Esther was faced with a dilemma. Xerxes did not know she was a Jew. If she said nothing about this matter to him, all her people would die. If she revealed her identity and asked that her people be spared, she might be killed too.

Esther's cousin Mordecai appealed to her to act. He said, "Who knows but that you have come to royal position for such a time as this?" (Esther 4:14). Who knows, Esther, if God has raised you up as queen for this very purpose, to save your people? The Bible tells us God gave Esther the courage to act, and she saved her people.

Like Esther, you and I tend to underestimate our significance. When we think of the countless worlds that make up the universe, we may see our world as just a small pebble compared to all the rest. When we think of the many years that make up human history, we may see ourselves as only one generation among many. When we think of the billions of people in the world, we may say, "I am only one person. What can I do?"

Yet God has a purpose for us, just as he had for Esther. He has placed us on Earth at this point in history for the purpose of glorifying him. With his help and with the talents he has given us, each of us is quite capable of contributing to his praise. In fact, by spreading the good news of our salvation, we may accomplish far more than we ever dreamed possible. Like Esther, we may save our people.

A matter of priorities

All of us have seen artists' sketches depicting space aliens with big bubble heads and small bodies with skinny arms and legs. Such sketches leave the impression that these beings have highly trained minds, but their physical development has been entirely neglected.

On the other hand, we may also have seen people who spend most of their lives down at the gym lifting weights. Their muscles bulge and ripple. They have necks as strong and thick as the average person's thigh. We marvel at their muscle development and physique. But what price have they paid? Have they perhaps concentrated so much on their physical development that they have neglected their mental development?

There is another side to man besides the mental and physical sides, however. There is also a spiritual side that needs development. The spiritual side of man—his relationship with God—needs attention. It needs to be given priority. Think of a well-balanced person who is athletic and articulate but doesn't know God. That person is a failure in God's eyes. He has neglected that part of his development which is most important of all. He is stunted spiritually. He is not living to glorify God. He has chosen to ignore God.

The world wants us to crowd our religion into a neat little compartment insulated from everyday life. Popular culture dictates that religion should be restricted to one hour on Sunday and should have absolutely no influence on life outside that one hour. The world's idea is that religion doesn't relate to real life. This is a world where people have to make a living. This is a world of power, money, and machines. God and religion don't fit in. The pressure to swallow such a secular way of thinking is relentless.

Secular humanism

One of the leading philosophies in our world is called *secular humanism*. To call something secular indicates it is concerned with earthly rather than spiritual matters. The word *humanism* reveals that this philosophy is centered on man. The principal concern of secular humanism is man—his relationship with himself, other people, and nature. Not all secular humanists are atheists, but the prevailing opinion among humanists is that whether God exists or not, man must live as though he didn't. Man's relationship with God is not important. Man has so many earthly needs, so many crises to solve in this world that he can't afford to turn his attention to God and the next world. Most secular humanists believe that God and religion distract people from concentrating on things of greater importance.

In the *Humanist Manifesto II*, issued in 1973, influential philosophers, scientists, educators, and psychologists set forth in summary form the most cherished principles of secular humanism. Among their statements were the following:

> Religions that place revelation, God, ritual, or creed above human needs and experience do a disservice to the human species.
>
> We can discover no divine purpose or providence for the human species.
>
> Humans are responsible for what we are or will become.
>
> No deity will save us; we must save ourselves.
>
> The human species is an emergence from natural evolutionary forces. There is no credible evidence that life survives the death of the body.
>
> Moral values derive their source from human experience.[1]

From just these few statements of this humanistic creed, it is easy to see that secular humanism is a blatant attempt by man to dethrone God. Though the Bible says God created man so that man might glorify and serve God (Isaiah 43:7), humanism says man should ignore God. Though the Bible says God has given us laws by which he commands us to live (John 14:15), humanism says man sets his own standards of right and wrong. Though the Bible says God will judge the world (Acts 17:31), humanism says man must determine his own actions. Man can control his own destiny.

Humanistic psychology

Sigmund Freud (1856–1939), a humanistic psychologist, has had great influence in the field of modern psychology. Freud believed that it is entirely natural for a criminal to act the way he does and that it is quite unreasonable for society to make a criminal stand trial for being his antisocial self. Furthermore, Freud did not believe man is responsible to any higher being. In fact, Freud considered all religious belief to be a neurotic illusion.

Freud's ideas laid the groundwork for the widespread denial of personal responsibility that abounds in modern American society. His influence led to the popular idea that people who commit crimes do so because of some experience or abuse they suffered in their childhood. Criminals, therefore, are not to be blamed. They are really victims of society. They are victims of their faulty upbringing and the weaknesses of the social systems around them. "Sin" is not in people but in the system. "Salvation" is not from God but is a matter of reordering or reeducating society. This lack of human responsibility, its attendant denial of guilt, and the idea of man's independence from God are recurring themes of humanism.

Abraham Maslow (1908–1970), another humanistic psychologist whose name is recognized by many people today, taught that morality is really a process of self-actualization. In other words, each person has internal qualities that should be allowed to develop naturally. According to Maslow, each person should be allowed to reach his unique potential by means of his own values and choices. Each person should determine for himself what is good or bad, right or wrong.[2] Maslow believed that it was unnecessary and even harmful to teach biblical morality. He also felt that morality and values must change as society changes. Maslow's opinion that man rather than God establishes morality is another recurring theme of humanism.

Modern psychology

Most modern psychologists are students of the humanistic psychologists who lived before them. That is why many psychologists today counsel their patients to deal with feelings of guilt by denying that they are responsible to God. They often tell their patients that they need not be concerned about the Ten Commandments. They tell their patients that if God does exist, he merely wants them to be happy. Therefore they need only to be true to themselves, following their own rules. Their own happiness ought to be their primary goal and ambition. Only one exception is made: they must be careful not to hurt others. However, even then, secular humanists tend to allow each person to determine whether his actions hurt others.

Our relationship with God

In contrast to the prevailing philosophy of secular humanism, we have seen that according to the Bible, man's relationship with God is of utmost importance. Man was created to enjoy a loving and personal relationship with God. Only when such a relationship exists can man be at peace and reach his full potential. Secular humanism turns the order of relationships around. Humanists say man must have a good relationship first with himself, then with others, then with nature.

But if the Bible teaches any lesson repeatedly, it is the importance of man's relationship with God and his complete dependence upon God. We see that lesson in the way the Old Testament presents the history of Israel. The Israelites grew into a mighty nation not because of their own efforts or because of mere accident but because God freed them from slavery in Egypt and blessed them.

Think of God's repeated warnings and encouragements that the Israelites might remain close to him, warnings given by Moses (Deuteronomy 4), Joshua (Joshua 24), Isaiah (Isaiah 1), and others. Whenever the Israelites fell away from God, they experienced nothing but trouble and misery.

Even kings of Israel, like Saul and Ahab, who thought they were above the law of God, felt the heavy hand of God's discipline, demonstrating that they were responsible to God. Saul came to a disgraceful end because he had forsaken God (1 Samuel 31:4). So did Ahab (1 Kings 21:19; 22:38). Not even kings could throw off the chains of God's commandments or oppose God successfully (Psalm 2:2-5). Again and again the lesson that every nation and every person is dependent on God and responsible to God is emphasized (Deuteronomy 17:14-20; 2 Kings 21:1-15; Isaiah 10:1-11; 13:1–23:18).

Thanks to God, there is a spiritual side to man so that man can know God and enjoy a loving, personal relationship with God. Thanks to God, man has a glorious spiritual purpose, to live to the glory of God. Thanks to God, there is a Savior who died on a cross to erase the times we have failed to carry out our God-given purpose. God has been good to us and is truly deserving of our highest praise.

2

The Glorious Importance of Man

Human worth can be measured in various ways. One way is to calculate the value of the chemical contents of the human body. With such an appraisal, an average person is worth only a few dollars at most. Another way to establish our worth is to consider what our employers pay us. According to our salaries, we may be worth a certain number of dollars an hour. Still another estimate might be offered by a financial planner, who would total all our assets to establish our net worth.

A more accurate appraisal of our worth would be the value God assigns to us. The creation account in Genesis demonstrates that our worth before God is considerable. The order in which God created everything testifies to the importance of man. Each step in creation prepared for the next. All previous steps in creation were made in preparation for man. Raymond Surburg speaks of the first three days as "days of preparation" and of the next three days as "days of accomplishment." Then he goes on to say:

> These days indicate the temporal order in which the creatures successively came into being, but they also contain a suggestion of rank in which the creatures stand to each other. The succeeding outrank the preceding creatures. The formless comes before the formed, the inorganic precedes the organic, the plants come before animals, and the animals precede man. Man is portrayed as the crown of creation.[3]

The crown of creation

The biblical creation account reveals that man was not merely the last of God's creatures; he was, as Surburg says, "the crown of creation." God created everything with man in mind. Everything else had to be finished first. There could not be the slightest omission or the smallest defect. Only when the earth was judged a perfect dwelling place was it ready for God's special creature, man.

When God said, "Let us make man in our image" (Genesis 1:26), he wasn't making a spur-of-the-moment decision or having an afterthought. Throughout his creation the all-knowing God was fully aware that he would create man. The prophet Isaiah says, "He who created the heavens, he is God; he who fashioned and made the earth, he founded it; he did not create it to be empty, but formed it to be inhabited" (Isaiah 45:18).

Made in God's image

Of all creation only man was made in the image of God. This too speaks of man's importance. It tells us man was created for a unique relationship with God, which none of the other visible creatures would have. Man was to be God's companion. With God's image man was given a knowledge of God that none of the creatures under man would have. He was given a will in agreement with God's will, righteous and holy (Ephesians 4:24).

Man did not have to compete with the animals for supremacy. God put man in charge of his creation. God said to Adam and Eve: "Be fruitful and increase in number; fill the earth and subdue it. Rule over the fish of the sea and the birds of the air and over every living creature that moves on the ground" (Genesis 1:28). All things, including all the vegetation and animals, were placed under man's rule. The psalmist said to God, "You made him [man] ruler over the works of your hands; you put everything under his feet" (Psalm 8:6).

Clearly, man was God's representative on earth. Man was the master of all the other creatures. They were commanded to render willing service to him. The whole earth was given to man to take care of, to rule, and to cultivate as a gardener tends his beloved garden. The Bible says, "The highest heavens belong to the LORD, but the earth he has given to man" (Psalm 115:16).

Man equal to the task

Was man capable of caring for God's world as God wanted? From the standpoint of intellect and insight, he certainly was. Consider Adam, standing in Paradise alone with God. All the beasts and birds were brought to him "to see what he would name them" (Genesis 2:19). Adam's ability to name God's creatures presupposes that Adam also had the ability to remember all the names he gave them. Since the fall into sin, it is questionable whether any of us would remember from one day to the next the names of even ten new animals we see for the first time. Adam named not just ten but all the animals and birds— and he remembered their names! Here was an intelligence far superior to that of anyone today!

Adam was indeed equal to his task of caring for the earth. His intelligence set him far above the creatures he ruled. His ability to communicate his thoughts and ideas was unparalleled in all God's visible creation. He was endowed with personality, feelings, and reasoning powers. He was far superior to almost all the other creatures God had made. Only the angels could claim greater power and ability. And being created in the image of God, man ruled God's world with a heart and mind perfectly in tune with God's will.

Furthermore, Adam was aware of his special position as the crown of God's creation. As Adam observed the various animals, he realized he was unique. None of the other creatures was like him. Among them "no suitable helper was found" (Genesis 2:20).

Further evidence of man's importance

By bringing all the animals and birds to Adam to name them, God awakened in Adam a longing for a companion who would be like him. Only after God had awakened that desire in Adam did he create Eve from a rib taken out of Adam. Eve was then brought to Adam and lovingly presented to him in a way that underscored Eve's importance and the importance of Adam and Eve's relationship. No such consideration was given to the animals or birds. They were simply placed together immediately, without any formal or informal introduction.

Man's importance also can be seen from the fact that when man fell into sin, the whole earth suffered. All creation shared man's fate under sin. Paul describes creation after the fall as "subjected to frustration" and "groaning as in the pains of childbirth" (Romans 8:20,22). Just as nations suffer under foolish and incompetent rulers, so the whole world began to suffer because of the sin and folly of man.

Further testimony to man's importance is that the Savior was sent to suffer and die for man but not for the animals. Heaven is described as a place for God, the angels, and man. We are never told whether animals will be in paradise. Apparently this is not important enough for us to know.

All that God tells us about man, from his creation to his future home in heaven, testifies to the dignity and glorious importance of man in God's sight, an importance far greater than that of the animals.

The unity of the human race

Did God create other human beings before or at the same time as Adam and Eve? The Bible states that before Adam "there was no man to work the ground" (Genesis 2:5). Paul expressly calls Adam "the first man" (1 Corinthians 15:45). From statements like these, we must conclude that there were no pre-Adamites. Also, there were no co-Adamites, or contemporaries of Adam. Paul traces all human beings back to Adam, saying, "From one man he [God] made every nation of men, that they should inhabit the whole earth" (Acts 17:26). Therefore all human beings must look to Adam as their ancestor.

What, then, is the origin of the different races? Today's racial variations result from the unfolding of the genetic potential Adam and Eve received from God at creation. It may be that God caused an acceleration in racial diversity after the flood, similar to the way he scattered mankind into different language groups at the tower of Babel (Genesis 11:1-9), but the Bible does not tell us this.

Today many secular anthropologists speculate that race is the result of a combination of three major influences: natural selection, environment, and inbreeding. Natural selection would favor those most able to survive and those most attractive to others. Environment would be responsible for such things as changes in skin color. Inbreeding would cause the gene pool to become more uniform, emphasizing some genetic traits while eliminating or suppressing others. Races are thought to be the result of small genetic changes that took place in isolated groups and breeding populations as natural selection, environment, and inbreeding influenced the gene pool.

Despite the existence of various races, secular anthropologists today have concluded that all people are of the same genus and species. So-called racial differences are only superficial. This conclusion agrees with the Scriptures, which indicate that all races and nationalities had their beginning in Adam. A major disagreement between secular anthropologists and the Bible regards how much time was required to account for racial differences. Secular anthropologists would generally argue for vast amounts of time, which biblical history does not allow.

The first woman

When we say Adam had no contemporaries, we are not denying the creation of Eve. But even Eve was not created independently of Adam. God did not form her from the dust of the ground and breathe into her the breath of life but formed her from a rib taken out of the man. She was not merely made of the same material as Adam; she was made *from* Adam. Eve also received the image of God (Genesis 1:27) and was given dominion over the creatures (verse 28). In everything she was Adam's partner. At the same time, when God created Adam first, he made woman subordinate to man (1 Timothy 2:11-13). He gave man and woman different responsibilities, and through sexual differences he fitted them for separate spheres of activity (Ephesians 5:22-33; 1 Corinthians 11:3-16; 14:34,35).

When God brought Eve to Adam, Adam was exuberant. He said, "This is now bone of my bones and flesh of my flesh" (Genesis 2:23). A more literal translation might be, "This one, this time is bone of my bones and flesh of my flesh." Though all the animals had paraded by, no suitable helper had been found for Adam. But this one, this time was!

Adam looked at Eve and saw blessings. Through Eve God gave Adam the blessing of companionship, someone with whom Adam could share his thoughts and feelings. Through Eve God gave Adam the blessings of sexual happiness and children. Just as Adam was special and one-of-a-kind, Eve was also special and of the same kind.

Evolution

Contrast all we have said thus far about man's importance to what evolution says about man. To the evolutionist, man is not at all special. He is merely a higher form of animal who evolved from lower forms of life over millions of years. Man has come from an amoeba. His closest relatives are the apes.

According to evolution, man is the product of chance, a gradual development from the very lowest form of life.

According to the Bible, man is the result of a loving God's creative act. God consulted with himself first, worked according to a plan, and then personally formed man from the dust of the ground and breathed into his nostrils the breath of life.

According to evolution, man began as a brute. According to the Bible, man was from the very beginning a super-intelligent creature, having a special relationship with God, and put in charge of God's creation.

Darwin's beliefs

In his *Origin of Species*, Charles Darwin (1809–1882) did not announce any intention to begin a crusade against the Bible. His goal was merely to present evidence that the species were not fixed and that all living things developed from simpler, original forms. Darwin even spoke of the Creator breathing life into a few forms.[4]

Whatever his intent may have been, Darwin laid the groundwork for the frontal assault on religion that would be made later by his followers. Darwin minimized the superiority of man over the animals. He emphasized whatever similarities he could discover, whether physical, social, or intellectual. To Darwin the similarities of man and the animals were far greater than the differences. He believed that men and animals had a common beginning and a common worth.

In his *Descent of Man*, Darwin made clear that he did not believe that conscience or moral sense came from God. He said, "The first foundation or origin of the moral sense lies in the social instincts, including sympathy; and these instincts no doubt were primarily gained, as in the case of the lower animals, through natural selection."[5]

Darwin denied that man has an instinctive belief in God. He was noncommittal about the soul.[6] And he stated that man should be excused for being proud of having risen from the depths and having in himself the potential to become even greater.[7] None of these ideas of Darwin are in harmony with the Bible.

No need for God

It should not surprise us that Darwin's followers would take his teachings to their inevitable conclusions. If evolution were true, there would be no need for an almighty, all-knowing God, no need for a supernatural Creator. And if there were no God, there would be no supernatural Being to whom we must answer. There would be no absolute right or wrong, since moral standards also would be a result of evolution, changeable and flexible. Sin would be an idea from which man must be liberated. The Savior himself would be unnecessary. Man would have no purpose on earth other than to live for himself and his own glory.

In spite of the dreary picture just painted, most people today accept the theory of evolution as an accurate account of man's origin. Though evolution is unproven in a scientific sense, the majority of public school science textbooks and popular encyclopedias present evolution as fact rather than theory. Objections to evolution are labeled "religious" or "philosophical" while evolution is considered scientific. Those who embrace evolution claim that the gaps still existing in our present knowledge of how evolution unfolded will be reduced or completely bridged as research progresses. Evolutionists believe it is only a matter of time before the theory of evolution is accepted by everyone.

Is compromise possible?

The idea of evolution has found a following even in some parts of the church. There are people in the church today who attempt to embrace both the idea of a personal, loving God and the idea of evolution. Those who believe that there is a God and that he used evolution to form this world are called theistic evolutionists, in contrast to atheistic evolutionists, who deny the existence of God.

But anyone who attempts to embrace both Christianity and evolution encounters very serious problems. The theistic evolutionist ends up with a trial-and-error god. His god is a tinkerer who continually experiments with his work, hoping finally to get it right. He is not the all-knowing and almighty God of the Scriptures, who can perform instantaneous miracles and for whom nothing is impossible (Matthew 19:26).

Evolution also calls into question the inspiration of Scripture. Whether one considers the time involved (millions of years or six days) or the manner in which man was formed (by chance or by a loving, all-knowing God), it is easy to see that evolution and Scripture simply do not agree. Surburg lists some 75 passages in the Bible that speak of the creative work of God.[8] Are we to discard all those passages? If the Bible is not true in its account of creation, how can we trust it when it tells us about Jesus and his saving work? Was Jesus really the Son of God and the Savior of the world? Or was he just another small ripple that once disturbed the sea of humanity?

People who accept evolution claim that the world and man are evolving into something better. But history has not shown this to be true. The improvements we have seen have all been superficial. They consist in a number of useful inventions that have improved the outward life of people but have not changed people themselves. Man's inhumanity to man continues. A beautiful new world of perfect people has failed to materialize. In fact, man is no more noble or moral today than in centuries past.

Man's superiority no accident

All of us have seen science fiction movies in which other creatures seized control of Earth. Generally through some laboratory accident or tragic nuclear disaster, people became the slaves of hideous mutants or cruel, diabolical beasts. We are grateful such movies are only a figment of Hollywood's imagination!

But in many anthropology textbooks, we are told in all seriousness that only due to evolutionary accident or pure chance, man, and not some other creature, is the master of this planet. If only a few pieces of the evolutionary puzzle had fallen together differently, we would be the ones living in zoos, and the animals would be our keepers!

The Bible, however, says God himself crowned man with glory and honor, giving him dominion over all the earth. God put all things under man's feet. God enabled man to raise and tend animals, sow and harvest crops, plant forests, and build hospitals. Man's abilities are not a mere accident; they are a gift of God.

The basis for our importance: God's love

According to the Bible, man's importance is undeniable. But the basis for man's value is not found in man's superior intelligence nor in man's ability to communicate or develop machines. Rather, it is found in the worth God has assigned us by his grace. When evolutionists celebrate their position as master of the universe, they express gratitude to chance and circumstance and pat themselves on the back. Christians, on the other hand, see their privileged place in creation as a gracious gift from a loving and caring God.

Furthermore, Christians see God's love and care reaching out not only to the human race as a group but also to each person. Jesus' parable of the lost sheep in Luke 15:3-7 describes God as a shepherd who has a hundred sheep. According to our cold and calculating way of thinking, the shepherd could afford to lose one sheep. But out of love he leaves the 99 in the open country to go after that one lost sheep. And he diligently searches for that sheep, not only until he is tired or until he can pride himself in his effort, but until he finds it. So great is the love of God that no sacrifice is too great for one soul! The conclusion might be drawn that even if you or I had been the only person to live, Jesus still would have come and given his life to rescue us.

Do you ever feel worthless? Does it ever seem as if no one really cares? Is your life not going as well as you had hoped and planned? Don't despair. Though all others forsake you, God will never forsake you. Jesus said not even a sparrow falls to the ground apart from the will of our heavenly Father. He assures us we are worth more than many sparrows. Even the very hairs of our heads are all numbered. We are important to God. We need not be afraid (Matthew 10:29-31).

3

Man's Glory Is Limited

An accurate estimate of human worth must avoid two extremes. One extreme was noted in the previous chapter, where we observed that evolution reduces man to nothing more than a highly developed animal. According to that point of view, man is a product of chance, without great significance and without eternal destiny. According to evolution, man has no loftier purpose than to satisfy his lowest instincts and appetites while he prepares the way for an animal higher on the evolutionary scale to succeed him.

The other extreme when measuring the worth of man is to identify man as divine. It may seem surprising that anyone would make that error. How could anyone confuse the clay with the potter, the finite with the infinite, the creature with the Creator? How could anyone fail to recognize the tremendous gulf that exists between man and God? Yet one philosopher after another and one religion after another have attempted the unthinkable. They have ascribed divinity to man.

Is man God?

What does the Bible say about man being God? From the Bible it is immediately apparent that God and man are distinct and separate beings. From Genesis we learn that God existed from eternity, but man had a beginning. Three times it is said in Genesis 1:27 that God created man, as if to emphasize that human beings are creatures of God, no more and no less. Man had no life of his own. God had to breathe into man's nostrils the breath of life. Man was made of dust and goes back to dust (Genesis 3:19). God is a spirit, without material substance, without flesh and bones (John 4:24).

The writer to the Hebrews marvels at God's goodness in crowning man with glory and honor and putting everything under his feet (2:7,8). Yet he also says God "made him [man] a little lower than the angels" (verse 7). If man is lower than the angels, who are mere created beings, how can man be God?

There is no encouragement in the Bible for any created being to entertain the hope of becoming God. Angels are not able to become God. When the angel we call Satan rebelled against God and set up a rival kingdom, pretending to be equal with God, he ensured his destruction (2 Peter 2:4; Jude 6). How, then, can man, who was made lower than the angels, expect to reach heights rebellious angels could not attain?

Only punishment for God's rivals

When Adam and Eve gave in to Satan's temptation to eat of the forbidden fruit in order to become wise like God, their punishment was swift and deadly. When Pharaoh challenged God and said, "Who is the LORD, that I should obey him and let Israel go?" (Exodus 5:2), God answered him with ten terrible plagues (Exodus 7–11). When Nebuchadnezzar became a god in his own eyes and failed to acknowledge the true God, he was stricken with insanity, "driven away from people and ate grass like cattle" (Daniel 4:33). When his descendant Belshazzar set himself up against the Lord of heaven, his punishment was announced by a hand writing on the wall. His days were numbered. He was weighed on the scales and found wanting. His kingdom was taken away (Daniel 5).

God has repeatedly threatened and brought punishment upon people when they aspire to become gods. This ought to be a powerful reminder to man neither to claim nor desire what he cannot have.

God is unique

In Isaiah 43 to 45, God points to himself no less than a dozen times as the only God. He says, "I am the LORD, and there is no other" (45:18). He claims to be the only Savior and invites everyone to trust in him (verses 21,22). He challenges us to suggest someone else who could do the deeds he does. He established the Israelites by freeing them from slavery in Egypt (Exodus 1–14). He fed them for 40 years with manna in the wilderness (Exodus 16; Deuteronomy 8:3,4). He helped Joshua defeat the Amorite kings by causing the sun to stand still (Joshua 10:1-14). He sent down fire from heaven to consume Elijah's offering after Baal and the false prophets failed to produce fire for their offering (1 Kings 18:16-46). Who else could intervene in history with such mighty deeds—and in the span of so many generations? God has divine attributes and abilities no one else has.

Predicting the future

A further proof of God's uniqueness and superiority is that only he can foretell the future with one hundred percent accuracy (Isaiah 44:7). In a striking demonstration of this ability, God foretold the name of the person who would bring Israel's Babylonian captivity to an end: Cyrus (verse 28). What makes this prediction especially remarkable is that it was made 90 years before the Babylonian captivity even began and 160 years before Cyrus gave permission for Israel to return from that exile. Such a prophecy would be similar to someone telling African people 160 years in advance that some of them would be sold into slavery in a place called America but that one day a man named Abraham Lincoln would set them free.

The ability to name Israel's deliverer 160 years in advance sets the God of the Bible apart as the one and only God. Only he could make a prediction like that. Only he can make astonishing predictions that always come true. By contrast, no human being exists who can predict the future with one hundred percent accuracy. What man foretells is only an educated guess or a mere stab in the dark.

There is no other!

Perhaps someone might argue that God's challenge in Isaiah 43 to 45 to match his deeds is really directed at the false gods of Israel's foreign neighbors. In other words, God is not denying that man is God but only that idols cannot be God. Yet God clearly says, "I am the LORD, and there is no other" (45:18). The "no other" not only includes the idols; it includes man.

When the Babylonians claimed a divine kingdom and said that it would continue forever (Isaiah 47:7) and when they mimicked God and said, "I am, and there is none besides me" (verse 8), God warned them of sudden destruction. When the ruler of Tyre said in his heart, "I am a god; I sit on the throne of a god in the heart of the seas," God replied, "You are a man and not a god" (Ezekiel 28:2). God vowed that Tyre too would be destroyed. The lesson in all this is clear: Every time man sets himself up as a god, he incurs punishment from the one and only true God.

Contrasting natures

Those who claim divinity for man ignore clear Scripture passages that emphasize the great contrast between the nature of God and the nature of man. Think of Isaiah's unforgettable vision of the Lord seated on his throne, surrounded by angels. When he saw God's glory, Isaiah said: "Woe to me! . . . I am ruined! For I am a man of unclean lips, and I live among a people of unclean lips, and my eyes have seen the King, the LORD Almighty" (Isaiah 6:5). Even when Isaiah's sin was purged, symbolized by a seraph (an angel) touching his lips with a live coal from the altar, he did not embrace the idea that he had reached the level of deity. Instead, he humbled himself before God and obeyed his commands.

When John had his vision of the new Jerusalem in Revelation 21, he said: "I heard a loud voice from the throne saying, 'Now the dwelling of God is with men, and he will live with them. They will be his people, and God himself will be with them and be their God" (verse 3). Far from being identified with God as God, the people in heaven are described as being in fellowship with God, while at the same time remaining distinct and separate beings. Even in heaven God is still the God of his people. Verse 7 promises that "he who overcomes will inherit all this, and I will be his God and he will be my son"—a flat contradiction that the destiny of the faithful is to be God.

The most popular god

None of this denies that man may set himself up as a false god. In his Large Catechism, Martin Luther once defined a god as "that to which your heart clings and entrusts itself."[9] In other words, your god is whatever is most important in your life or whatever you look to for the greatest blessings, help, and comfort. If we asked people to name the most popular false god in the world today, some might suggest Allah, Buddha, or Brahman. Still others might say the most popular false god is money, pleasure, or popularity. But isn't it because people are devoted to themselves above all else that their own comfort and pleasure are so important to them? There is no doubt that the greatest false god today is self. Behind people's love for money and other possessions is the idolatry of self.

It has been said that 20th-century man worships six gods: self, money, fame, power, pleasure, and knowledge. When we hear that accusation, our immediate reaction might be to defend ourselves. We don't worship any of those things, do we? But every year statistics show that people in the United States spend considerably more money on cosmetics or on their pets than they give to churches for the work of the Lord. When people choose recreation on Sunday mornings instead of church, what is that but self-worship? When people gossip about others so they themselves look good, what is that but a form of self-worship?

Playing God

We have seen that divinity is not attainable for man. Yet people delight in acting as if they were god. An example of this is cursing. We know that only God has the right or power to damn someone. God decides who goes to heaven and who goes to hell. But how often puny human beings utter curses, damning their hammer, their dog, or their neighbor. Clearly, they are playing God! They are saying: "Move over, God. *I'm* going to damn a few." Or even worse, if that's possible, they are ordering God to do their bidding. They are snapping their fingers and saying: "C'mon, God! Come on down and do your trick! I want you to damn my hammer, God. Damn my dog. Damn my neighbor. You'd better do it! I'm telling you, God!" No wonder God has forbidden us to curse.

In recent years man has experienced tremendous success in technology and medicine. No longer does any problem seem insurmountable for the human race. No longer does any invention appear to be beyond man's capability. Assuming that man has enough time and that he expends enough effort, he is confident he can solve any dilemma. The trend in our society is complete self-reliance. Not only does man feel he does not need God, he dares to take God's place in deciding who will live and who will die. The struggle for abortion and euthanasia are nothing but thinly veiled attempts to play God.

God doesn't make fun of us

Many parents today are saddened when they send their children away to college at great cost to themselves only to find that their children have learned to despise them, their values, and their faith. Steeped in secular culture and learning, young adults tend to exaggerate their own intelligence and importance to the world, and they often underestimate the worth of their parents. The young make fun of those who are getting older because their memory isn't as good as it used to be or because they tell the same stories over and over again or because their clothing is hopelessly out of date or because they hobble around with a cane.

Similarly, every one of us, young or old, could be ridiculed by God. How little we know, compared to what God knows! How little we remember! What little we can do! How slowly we move around this planet. How feeble our efforts in overcoming sin! How laughable we must be to God! How ripe for ridicule! But God does not make fun of us. He loves us and treats us with respect. But when we seek to throw him off his throne and take his place, he moves to discipline us. Then he says: "I am the LORD; that is my name! I will not give my glory to another or my praise to idols" (Isaiah 42:8).

The New Age Movement

In January 1987 actress Shirley MacLaine, appearing on the Johnny Carson show, shouted: "I am God! I am God! I am God!" She went on to tell her television viewers they too were God. Together with God they had created the world. In themselves resided all wisdom and the answers to all questions. If only each person would become more aware of his divinity, the world's problems would cease!

Where did MacLaine get such ideas? From the New Age Movement she was helping to popularize. Also called the human potential movement and the Age of Aquarius, the New Age Movement began here in the United States in the 1970s. During that decade thousands of young people, burnt out on the drugs and militant politics of the 1960s, tried to find answers in cults and Eastern religions.

The result was that they began to embrace many Hindu ideas. One such idea is that man is part of God.

New Age beliefs

Though not all New Agers agree in everything, a few beliefs are accepted by all of them. For example, all New Agers accept monism, the idea that all is one. In other words, everything that exists consists of one and the same essence, or reality. New Agers believe this ultimate reality is not just dead matter but force, energy, being, awareness, consciousness, and bliss. Whatever the god of the New Age is called, it is an impersonal god, a god that cannot hear when spoken to.

The two basic beliefs that all is one and that God is impersonal are followed naturally by two others: all that is, is God (pantheism) and man, as part of all that is, is God. These are the principal beliefs of all disciples of the New Age Movement and the chief doctrines of Hinduism. None of these teachings are scriptural.

Man not accountable to God

As a result of their belief in man's divinity, New Agers do not see that man's purpose in life is to glorify God but, rather, that man might realize he himself is God. Man's purpose is to achieve his divine potential. Man must learn to rely on himself rather than on some God outside himself. According to New Age teaching, the only authority man needs to follow is the inner light of his "higher self." Man is accountable only to himself.

Almost all New Agers accept the Hindu beliefs of reincarnation and karma. The law of karma states that every thought, word, and action brings about specific and proportionate consequences. Since most people cannot pay off in

one lifetime all the bad consequences they have accumu-
lated because of their bad deeds, they must return by reincarnation until all their bad karma is balanced by good
karma. By successive incarnations, sooner or later everyone
reaches the highest level. From there man can escape the
cycle of incarnations and finally merge with God.

New Age enlightenment

An important goal of the New Age Movement is to
enlighten man to the truth that he is God. To produce that
enlightenment in themselves and to focus on their inner
strength and divinity, New Agers use methods such as self-
hypnosis, yoga, and transcendental meditation. Sometimes
the unsuspecting are exposed to these activities as an introduction to New Age teachings. For example, the practice
of transcendental meditation was introduced into the New
Jersey public school system in 1975 and financed by the
federal government. This practice lasted a short time. As
another example, representatives of some of the United
States' largest corporations, including IBM, AT&T, and
General Motors, met in New Mexico in the summer of
1985 to discuss how Hindu mysticism might help execu-
tives improve their work performance.

One of the most disturbing practices followed by many
in the New Age Movement is channeling. Channelers are
mediums, people who claim to communicate with those
who lived in the past or even with beings from outer space.
Perhaps the most famous channeler is J. Z. Knight, a
woman who supposedly communicates with Ramtha, a
fierce warrior who lived about 35,000 years ago. According
to Knight, Ramtha evolved through reincarnation into a
wise and good man who is willing to share all the truth he
has learned about the universe for $200 per hour. If Knight

had practiced channeling in Old Testament Israel, she would not have become wealthy. Instead, she would have been stoned to death at God's command (Leviticus 20:27).

Basic differences between the Bible and the New Age Movement

Bible	New Age Movement
God is a supreme personal being, separate and distinct from his creation (Genesis 1:27; Job 38:4).	God is an impersonal force or awareness, the sum of all that exists.
Man is God's special creature, made in God's image and responsible to God's holy law (Genesis 1:27; 2:16,17).	Man is god, responsible only to himself.
Jesus Christ is the unique God-man (2 Corinthians 4:5; John 3:16).	Jesus Christ is God, but no more God than anyone else.
Man's greatest problem is sin, which separates man from God and makes God angry with him (Isaiah 59:2; Romans 1:18).	Man's greatest problem is ignorance of his divinity.
Sin is atoned for by the substitutionary suffering and death of Jesus Christ (Isaiah 53:5,6; 2 Corinthians 5:21).	Sin (bad karma) is compensated for in future lives; man saves himself.
Man dies once and after death faces judgment (Hebrews 9:27).	Man undergoes a series of reincarnations before finally merging with God.
The ultimate truth is to be found only in the Bible (Isaiah 8:20; Revelation 22:18,19).	Truth can be found in man's inner consciousness by meditation, reading other "holy books" besides the Bible, or channeling through mediums.

The Mormons

Besides the New Age Movement, an organized religious group, spawned in the United States, also teaches the deity of man. That group is the Mormons, or the Church of Jesus Christ of Latter-day Saints. Mormons are generally pro-family, good citizens, and morally upright, and they avoid anything that might adversely affect their health, such as tobacco, alcohol, and caffeine. But although Mormons have much to commend them, their teachings leave much to be desired. In brief, here is what they teach about God and man:

> In the beginning, the head of the Gods called a council of the Gods; and they came together and concocted a plan to create the world and people it.[10]

> God himself was once as we are now, and is an exalted man.[11]

> As man is, God once was: as God is, man may become.[12]

> We are in the same relation to him [God] as a tiny infant is to an earthly parent. Though comparatively weak and helpless, the child nevertheless possesses the seeds of character and the embryonic capacity to attain to all the powers and virtues of maturity. These capacities will expand and grow as he faces life's experiences. . . . As God's children we have in us the seeds of Godhood.[13]

From these statements we see that Mormons deny the doctrine of the Trinity. They have many gods, not just one god. They teach that man can become a god. To reach deity a person must faithfully obey the laws of the Mormon church. The gods are a family any Mormon can join through determined effort.

Satan's lie

It is good for us to remember who first taught that man can become God. Satan did that when he tempted Adam and Eve. Satan lied when he told them, "You will be like God" (Genesis 3:5). Adam and Eve believed the lie and ushered in the reign of sin and death. Satan's lie was harmful and deadly then and is still harmful and deadly today.

Those who have the truth concerning the identity and worth of man are those who accept what the Bible says about these matters. We must resist the prompting of our pride to think more highly of ourselves than we ought. As glorious as man is, his glory is still limited.

A proper balance

It bears repeating that an accurate estimate of human worth must avoid the two extremes of worthlessness and pride. Because we so often vacillate between such feelings, someone once suggested we should carry two stones in our pockets. On one should be written, "I am but dust and ashes." On the other should be written, "For my sake the world was created." When we are filled with pride, thinking we are God or we don't need God, we should look at the stone that says, "I am but dust and ashes." When we are troubled by feelings of worthlessness, we should look at the stone that says, "For my sake the world was created." In each case we might be brought back to reality.

We humans are not God. We are not even close to being God. We will never be God. Our glory is limited. We are, however, the crown of God's creation. We are dearly loved by God and are objects of his grace and tender mercy. The more we understand what a blessing *that* is, the more we will be content with who we are.

4

A Closer Look at What Makes Man Glorious

Parents who love their children are fond of telling them they are special. It may be the child's blue eyes or happy personality. It may be the child's status in the family, the oldest or the youngest. It may be the child's special ability in reading or math. Whatever makes children unique or exceptional, loving parents make sure they know they are special.

God gave us a glorious body

Our heavenly Father wasted no opportunity to show us we are special to him. God's greatest demonstration of love was sending his Son to die for the sins of the world. But God also demonstrated his love by giving us bodies that are unique and special among his creatures.

Human hands are so adept and nimble that a concert pianist can play hundreds of notes in a minute. The human body is made up of more than six hundred muscles that cross one another or are imbedded in one another, enabling a gymnast to perform amazing tumbling feats. The human mind is so versatile that no computer program has been developed yet that can perform all the mind's functions. Communication skills enable humans to share ideas and to learn what others have known before them.

The eye and the heart

Think of the human eye. When visual cells called rods and cones gather light, a chemical reaction takes place that sends messages to the brain by way of nerves. This creates the sensation of light in the mind and results in the three-dimensional pictures we see of the world around us. The eye has the marvelous ability to adjust its focus automatically according to the distance of the object it sees. It adapts to the presence of bright lights or darkness.

Or think of the human heart. In a year's time, the heart will pump about 40 million times without being told to pump. It knows when to pump fast and when to slow down. About four thousand gallons of blood pass through the heart daily. That is 450,000 tons in the average lifetime. The average human body has 75,000 miles of blood vessels. The heart moves that river of blood day after day and night after night without stopping. Though the heart is a very effective pumping machine, it weighs only about 12 ounces. No wonder the psalmist says to God, "I praise you because I am fearfully and wonderfully made; your works are wonderful" (Psalm 139:14).

Man's precious soul

The gift of a specially prepared body did not exhaust God's generosity toward man. God also gave man a precious soul. The Bible speaks of the soul as such a priceless possession that its loss would be an incalculable tragedy. Jesus said, "What good is it for a man to gain the whole world, yet forfeit his soul? Or what can a man give in exchange for his soul" (Mark 8:36,37).

But what is a soul? Perhaps the best way to begin answering that question is to say the soul makes man different from everything else God created. Man has height, size, and weight. So does a rock. Man takes in nourishment and grows. So does a tree. Man feels and moves about. So does a dog. But man has one thing no other creature has: a soul, which enables man to think spiritual thoughts and perform spiritual actions. The soul is the spiritual part of man.

Man's soul is rational. It can think and reason. Because man has a rational soul with will and emotions, in contrast to an animal's instincts, man can enter into an intimate relationship with God, which animals cannot do. In fact, as we saw in Chapter 1, this is why God created man as he did, so that man could have fellowship with God and be his companion for all eternity.

The Bible credits the soul with intelligence. For example, Psalm 77:6 says, "My spirit [synonym for soul] inquired." Making an inquiry is a sign of intelligence. Therefore the soul (spirit) is intelligent. The Bible also credits the soul with emotions (Psalm 42:5) and the ability to love God and others (Luke 10:27). It points to the soul as the carrier of man's personality and conscious self. For example, when the psalmist says, "My soul refused to be comforted" (Psalm 77:2), he means, "I refused to be comforted." Therefore, the soul is "me," man's personality and conscious self. Above all, the Bible credits the soul with the ability and desire to give praise and thanks to God. For example, David tells how his soul will respond when God delivers him from his enemies: "My soul will rejoice in the LORD and delight in his salvation" (Psalm 35:9).

The soul gives life

No one has ever seen electricity, but we know electricity exists because of what it does. Similarly, no one has ever seen a soul. Yet we know the soul exists because of its activities. The fact that it gives life to the body testifies to its existence. Even more important is the testimony of Scripture. From the Bible we know that the soul is just as real as our hands and feet, even though it cannot be seen and it takes up no space in our bodies.

Because the soul gives life to the body, one might compare the soul to a battery that gives life and action to a child's toy. When the battery is removed, the toy's action ceases. When the soul leaves the body, the body loses its power and life. But the soul-body relationship is not one-sided. Just as the body needs the soul to live, so the soul needs the body to carry out its will. The relationship of body and soul is one of mutual dependence.

The soul's immortality

Though the body can die, the soul cannot. The soul lives forever. No one can strangle it, cut it up, drown it, or mow it down with bullets. The soul is immortal, giving us life that will never end. When our bodies die, our souls leave our bodies and return to God to be judged (Ecclesiastes 12:7; Hebrews 9:27).

The fact that the body perishes while the soul lives on ought to be a powerful reminder to us to take special care of our souls. Many people today spend most of their energy taking care of their bodies—from the vitamins they take in the morning to the orthopedic mattresses they sleep on at night. But when this life is over, only one thing will matter: the care we have given our souls. Only souls that receive proper nourishment from God's Word will be safe. Only souls that trust in Christ will receive the wonderful invitation "Come, you who are blessed by my Father; take your inheritance, the kingdom prepared for you since the creation of the world" (Matthew 25:34).

Origin of the soul

Exactly how do we receive our souls? Directly from God? From our parents? Or by some other way? Through the years theologians have proposed the following four theories concerning the origin of the soul:

1. *Emanationism:* This theory states the soul is an emanation of God rather than a creation of God. In other words, the soul is part of God's essence, or being, that he has sent forth, rather than a living entity created outside God. Having already addressed the idea that man is God (Chapter 3), we will not discuss this theory at length here. Those who insist on claiming that the soul is part of God might well ponder what Paul says in 2 Corinthians 7:1, where he urges us to "purify ourselves from everything that contaminates body and spirit." If the soul (here called the spirit) were part of God, then this passage would be suggesting an obvious impossibility, namely, that the holy God himself could be contaminated. Remember that the Bible also states God will destroy the souls of unbelievers in hell (Matthew

10:28). If the soul were part of God, we would be asked to accept the absurdity that God will destroy part of his own essence in hell.

2. *Preexistantism:* This theory assumes all souls were created in the beginning. As human conception occurs, one of those ready souls is sent into the new body. This theory has not been taught by Lutherans. There is no support in Scripture for it.

3. *Creationism:* This theory assumes God creates a soul *directly* for every new body. In creating the soul, God does not use human parents in any way. Those who defend this theory find support in Bible passages that say God gives the soul to man (Ecclesiastes 12:7; Zechariah 12:1) and God is "the Father of our spirits" (Hebrews 12:9).

4. *Traducianism:* This theory holds that God creates the soul in the same way he creates the body: he uses human parents. The new soul is generated, or propagated, with the body in conception. Those who defend this theory find support in the Bible passage that states a descendant lives in his father's body before conception (Hebrews 7:10).

Lutheran theologians generally have considered this topic an open question (a question the Bible doesn't answer definitively one way or another) and have allowed for the possibility of either creationism or traducianism. However, many Lutheran theologians have expressed a preference for traducianism. In their opinion this theory best explains original sin. In their opinion creationism makes God responsible for creating something sinful, since the soul is sinful from its beginning. Traducianism, on the other hand, looks upon original sin as something transferred to the soul from human parents.

This is in keeping with the Bible, which says sin and death came upon all people through Adam (Genesis 5:1-3; Romans 5:12).

Dichotomy or trichotomy?

Another point of controversy that has engaged theologians for centuries is whether man consists of two chief parts, body and soul (*dichotomy*), or three parts: body, soul, and spirit (*trichotomy*). According to trichotomy, the soul is a lower principle of life that man has in common with animals. The spirit is a higher, or spiritual, principle that distinguishes man from animals.

Bible passages used to support trichotomy are not conclusive. For example, it is true that Mary refers to both "soul" and "spirit" in Luke 1:46,47: "My soul glorifies the Lord and my spirit rejoices in God my Savior." But it does not logically follow that because the Bible uses both terms, we should conclude soul and spirit are different from one another. When we understand the parallelism of Hebrew poetry, which Mary employs in this verse, we realize Mary is saying the same thing twice. It is customary in Hebrew poetry to repeat the same thought with slightly different words. Therefore, Mary's words are actually evidence that *soul* and *spirit* are synonymous.

In the Bible those who have died are called either spirits (1 Peter 3:19) or souls (Revelation 6:9), further evidence that the Bible uses the terms *spirit* and *soul* interchangeably, indicating they are identical. Dichotomy is also supported by Matthew 10:28: "Do not be afraid of those who kill the body but cannot kill the soul. Rather, be afraid of the One who can destroy both soul and body in hell." Man is described in totality. His whole being is cut off from the eternal life-giving blessings of God. And what constitutes man's whole being? Only two parts: body and soul. Solomon's description of death also portrays man as made of two parts: "The dust returns to the ground it came from, and the spirit returns to God who gave it" (Ecclesiastes 12:7).

The image of God

God gave man a glorious body and mind with skills that none of the other creatures possessed. He also gave man a precious soul, which enables man to think spiritual thoughts and to live forever. Only man has a soul. A third gift not shared by the other creatures was that God made man in his own image. This was the greatest gift of all, and it set man even farther above the other creatures.

When God discussed the creation of man in Genesis 1, God did not say, "Let us give man a glorious body" or "Let us give man a precious soul." Instead, he said, "Let us make man in our image, in our likeness, and let them rule over the fish of the sea and the birds of the air, over the livestock, over all the earth" (verse 26). Before he created man, God singled out the one gift that would make man especially glorious, compared to all God's other creatures. Man would be made in the image of God.

God's image: righteousness and holiness

Since God is a spirit (he has no body), the image of God cannot be anything physical. Instead, it has to do with the intellect, will, and emotions of man's soul. Furthermore, at creation this blessing of God's image was not merely that man was a superior rational being who could think and plan better than animals but especially that man's intellect and will were rightly disposed toward God.

Therefore, the image of God has sometimes been called the state of integrity or the state of innocence.

The apostle Paul helps us understand what makes up the image of God when he compares it with the natural sinful state of man as he is born into the world. Paul told the Ephesians: "You were taught . . . to put off your old self, which is being corrupted by its deceitful desires; to be made new in the attitude of your minds; and to put on the new self, created to be like God in true righteousness and holiness" (4:22-24). Paul calls the image of God, which was being restored in the Ephesians, the new self. Notice that according to Paul, the image of God has to do with one's attitude, one's way of thinking and feeling (which also determines how one will act). The two words characterizing the attitude of the new self are righteousness and holiness.

God's image: knowledge

In his letter to the Colossians, Paul gives us further insight into this special gift of God's image: "[You] have put on the new self, which is being renewed in knowledge in the image of its Creator" (3:10). Here we see that the image of God also consists of knowledge, not that at creation Adam's knowledge was a carbon copy of God's knowledge or that Adam knew everything God knew. Man is always limited in his knowledge; God is omniscient. Man is always the creature; God is the creator.

For Adam and Eve, the gift of God's image meant their knowledge and thinking ran parallel to God's in respect to righteousness and holiness. They knew God's will and found joy and satisfaction in following that will. They also knew God himself in a righteous and holy way. They knew intuitively that God was kind and loving. They trusted

God's goodness and enjoyed his presence. Only when Adam and Eve sinned and lost the image of God did they hide in the garden out of fear of God. As long as they possessed God's image, they had a unique relationship with God that none of the other creatures had. They were God's companions.

God's image: success and happiness

Have you ever wondered what it would be like to succeed at everything you try, to have the wisdom to make only right decisions, and to have the stamina and fortitude to carry out those decisions? For us today such aspirations are unrealistic. But not for Adam and Eve. They were perfect human beings who had the ability to achieve goals toward which you and I can only aspire.

Created in the image of God, Adam and Eve had the wisdom and desire to use everything in this world in a God-pleasing way, to harness every law of nature to the glory of God. They were holy and without sin. What beautiful and happy people they must have been as God's perfect representatives and his loving companions! They were a success not only in their own eyes but also in God's.

Gifts for a purpose

Having taken a closer look at the various gifts of God that made man glorious, let's not forget that God gave all these gifts for a purpose: that man might glorify God and center his life on God. Man's marvelous body testified to the goodness of God and gave man a powerful reason to find God and thank him for that gift. Man's soul enabled him to think spiritual thoughts, to know God, and to live forever. The image of God made man righteous and holy, enabling him to approach God and be God's intimate companion. Every one of God's gifts to man furthered God's purpose of having a loving, personal relationship with man.

A *glorious beginning*

This brings us to the close of the first part of our story of God's beloved creature man. We have been reminded of man's glorious beginning. We have seen how wonderfully man was made: with a special body and mind, with a precious soul, and even in the very image of God. We have also reviewed the special purpose for which man was made: to have a loving and intimate companionship with God.

What joy there must have been among the angels of God as they gazed upon man, the crown of God's creation! What admiration they must have felt for God, who had made such a beautiful and perfect creature! What anticipation they must have felt! How happy God must have been to see the fruits of his labor and to anticipate a loving fellowship with his glorious creature man!

Would man live up to all these expectations? Would he remain the glorious creature God intended him to be? Sadly, as our story continues, we find a great tragedy awaiting man, a tragedy he will bring upon himself.

Part II

Ashes

5

Man Plays with the Fire of Sin

It's a tragedy all too common in our society. A young child finds a book of matches or a cigarette lighter and begins to play with it. The child is fascinated by it and completely unaware of the danger of his new "toy." He has never played with anything like this before. But the child's curiosity and excitement are soon replaced with fear and a sense of panic because his newfound "friend" quickly turns against him. In no time at all, fire engulfs the room in which he is playing and spreads throughout the entire house. In a matter of minutes, the house is nothing but ashes, and all the people inside are dead.

In the worst tragedy that ever happened to the human race, Adam and Eve lit the match that engulfed the world in the flames of sin and killed all its occupants. But unlike the child who plays with matches unawares, Adam and Eve were not ignorant. God had plainly warned them, "You are free to eat from any tree in the garden; but you must not eat from the tree of the knowledge of good and evil, for when you eat of it you will surely die" (Genesis 2:16,17).

No excuse

Adam and Eve had no excuse to sin. If God had placed them in a barren wasteland or desert where they had nothing to eat or drink or if God had given them bodies that hurt or didn't function properly or if they were in constant physical danger, someone might suggest they had reason to doubt God's goodness or question God's motives when he gave his command. But everything was absolutely perfect. Adam and Eve were in a beautiful garden where they lacked nothing. Nothing they knew and nothing they had experienced indicated God was unkind or worthy of disobedience.

When Satan appeared to Eve in the form of a serpent, he said, "Did God really say, 'You must not eat from any tree in the garden'?" (Genesis 3:1). Satan's intent was to cast doubt on God's goodness and the truthfulness of his Word. How could God be so mean? How could he be so cruel? Surely he would not deny Adam and Eve the pleasure of eating the fruit of a tree in the garden!

Instead of immediately recoiling at the suggestion of unkindness in God, Eve carefully mulled over Satan's question in her mind. She also continued her conversation with Satan. By doing so, Eve gave Satan the opportunity to plant seeds of doubt in her mind about God's truthfulness and goodness. Satan offered no proof that his word should be believed over God's, nor did Eve demand any proof. She had no excuse for believing Satan instead of God.

Judging God

Today too, how quickly people set themselves up as judges over God's Word! Has God really said what he said? And if so, is God's Word the last word on the matter? Many feel they cannot simply accept everything the Bible says without subjecting it to human reason, human experience, and scientific investigation. Many feel they are fully capable of critically evaluating God's motives, character, and abilities. Many pass judgment on God. They accept evolution. They deny the miracles and deity of Christ. They accept almost without question whatever science says, but what God says is doubted, criticized, corrected, and even laughed at.

God's fault?

Some actually believe that Adam and Eve's fall into sin was God's fault. They believe God should have known what would happen and should have prevented the fall. Either he should not have given Adam and Eve the free will to choose between obedience and sin, or he should not have forbidden them to eat of the tree.

Certainly, the God who blessed Adam and Eve so bountifully and later sacrificed his only Son for mankind needs no defense. But for the sake of argument, why should we conclude God was unkind because he gave Adam and Eve a free will? Would they have been happier if they had been puppets or constructed like robots or mechanical toys? God in his love and wisdom determined that human beings would be happier if their obedience was voluntary rather than forced.

We must remember that even with a free will, it certainly was possible for man not to sin. As we learned in Chapter 4, Adam and Eve were created in the image of God. They had an intuitive knowledge of what God was like, that he was kind, loving, and trustworthy. Their wills were in perfect harmony with God's will. They were not predisposed toward sin. The suggestion to sin came from outside them. It could not come from within as long as they were in the state of innocence.

An opportunity to say thank you

But wasn't it a mistake for God to tell Adam and Eve not to eat of the forbidden tree? Didn't that command of God make God partly responsible for the fall into sin? That charge is sometimes leveled against God.

God's command should be considered an act of kindness. Suppose one person is very generous toward another, lavishing gifts on every occasion. And suppose that when the person who is inundated with gifts attempts to give a small gift in return, it is refused. Or suppose there is no way to say thank you. Suppose there is only the possibility of accepting gifts and never a way to show gratitude for those gifts. Wouldn't that be an uncomfortable situation?

It is far more satisfying for someone who is filled with gratitude to have at least some small way to express that gratitude. Such an opportunity to say thank you was what God gave Adam and Eve when he told them there was one thing they should do for him: refrain from eating from the tree of the knowledge of good and evil in the middle of the garden.

But even more was at stake than just an occasion to say thank you. God's command gave Adam and Eve another opportunity to fulfill the purpose for which they had been created. Luther pointed out that the tree of the knowledge of good and evil was Adam and Eve's "church, altar, and pulpit."[14] There they were to fulfill their purpose of worshiping God, freely yielding the obedience they owed, and giving thanks to God. God's command to avoid the forbidden tree was an opportunity to glorify God by consciously choosing good over evil. If they chose good, they would live forever. If they chose evil, they would die.

The fall

After the initial temptation, when Satan realized Eve was beginning to doubt God's fairness in commanding her not to eat of the tree, Satan decided he could directly contradict what God had said. Here follows the simple and tragic account of what happened:

> "You will not surely die," the serpent said to the woman. "For God knows that when you eat of it your eyes will be opened, and you will be like God, knowing good and evil." When the woman saw that the fruit of the tree was good for food and pleasing to the eye, and also desirable for gaining wisdom, she took some and ate it. She also gave some to her husband, who was with her, and he ate it. Then the eyes of both of them were opened, and they realized they were naked; so they sewed fig leaves together and made coverings for themselves. Then the man and his wife heard the sound of the LORD God as he was walking in the garden in the cool of the day, and they hid from the LORD God among the trees of the garden. But the LORD God called to the man, "Where are you?" He answered, "I heard you in the garden, and I was afraid because I was naked; so I hid." And he said, "Who told you that you were naked? Have you eaten from the tree that I commanded you not to eat from?" The man said, "The woman you put here with me—she gave me some fruit from the

tree, and I ate it." Then the LORD God said to the woman, "What is this you have done?" The woman said, "The serpent deceived me, and I ate." (Genesis 3:4-13)

The temptation Satan presented was not only an attack on God's truthfulness; it questioned his love. Satan put God's prohibition in an ugly light. Satan pictured Adam and Eve's great benefactor as selfish and envious. He claimed God was trying to keep something good and desirable from them. John Jeske paraphrases Satan's lie this way: "God has forbidden you to eat the fruit only because he knows eating it would endow you with a secret knowledge, the knowledge that you can live without God. Eve, God doesn't want you to discover the tremendous potential that lies in your human reason. Instead he wants to keep you ignorant."[15]

When Eve heard that, she became as fascinated with the fruit of the forbidden tree as a child is fascinated with matches or a cigarette lighter. Just as fire can be attractive and exciting to a child, so Eve found the fruit of that tree to be good, pleasing, and desirable. She wanted to know what God knew. She wanted to be like God. But the end results of her eating were disappointing. She lost goodness and was guilty of evil. And the same was true of her husband when he joined her in eating. Together they suffered shame and fear, loss of innocence, and the onset of death and destruction.

A fall upwards?

Various heathen philosophers have claimed that Adam and Eve's fall into sin was actually good for mankind. Georg Hegel, Friedrich von Schiller, Erich Fromm, and Pierre Teilhard de Chardin are among those who have claimed that the fall was beneficial. Hegel thought a knowledge of evil was necessary so that man could understand good. Schiller actually called the fall "the happiest and greatest event in human history."[16] His reasoning was that the fall marked the beginning of freedom for man. From this time on, man would begin to determine his own morality. Only in this way, by striking out on his own, would man be able to reach his greatest potential. Fromm also considered the fall man's first step toward freedom. Teilhard de Chardin spoke of it as a necessary part of the evolutionary process. But these are only restatements of Satan's lie to Adam and Eve when he claimed that sin would have benefits.

The Bible leaves no doubt that the fall into sin was an absolute disaster. Adam and Eve immediately and for the first time in their lives felt shame regarding their nakedness. They were ashamed of the bodies God had given them. They realized they were no longer in full control of their sexual desires. In every respect they were unhappy with themselves. Their consciences told them they were not the pure and holy beings they once had been.

Ruined relationships

Adam and Eve's relationships with God, each other, and nature were ruined. Their relationship with God was ruined. Before they sinned, they had felt joy in the presence of God, but after they sinned, they ran from him in fear and thought they could hide. They even tried to blame God for their fall. Adam blamed God for giving him the woman, and Eve blamed God for creating the serpent.

The relationship between Adam and Eve also was ruined. The perfect harmony that had existed between them was gone. The same man who had once praised Eve as his perfect companion accused her of destroying his life. He was selfish and without pity. Love for his neighbor was replaced by an all-consuming love of self. The headship of a sinful and selfish husband would not be pure joy to his wife.

Man's relationship with nature also was shattered. His dominion over nature was curtailed. The ground was cursed. Tending it was hard work.

Adam and Eve were weakened physically and made subject to pain, sickness, and death. Childbirth was extremely painful. Mental sharpness was dulled. Having lost their state of innocence, Adam and Eve were no longer completely free of psychological problems. Life became a struggle (Genesis 3:16-19).

Added to these sufferings was the fact that Adam and Eve were expelled from the beautiful garden that had been their home. They were driven out lest they eat of the tree of life and live forever in their sin-stained condition (Genesis 3:22-24). The losses they suffered, the shame they felt, the pain that lay ahead of them—all these bitter consequences prove that the fall into sin was not a fall upwards but the greatest calamity that would ever come upon man.

Blaming God

When Adam blamed the woman God gave him, he implied that if God had given him a better companion, he would not have fallen. When Eve blamed the serpent, she implied that if God had made the serpent a little less clever, she would not have been misled. Both of them agreed that God was the one responsible for their fall. But by blaming God both of them were avoiding the one action they most needed to take. They needed to repent of what they had done.

It shouldn't surprise us that Adam and Eve would try to wiggle out from under their predicament by blaming someone else. People still do the same thing today. When people get themselves into trouble, they often try to shift the blame. They say the fault is not in them or their sinful actions but in society or the environment. Or they say the problem was caused by their parents. Some even blame God. God should have made them richer; then they wouldn't have been tempted to steal. God should have given them a better marriage partner; then they wouldn't have been unfaithful. But such shifting of blame is no more helpful today than after the fall. It leads people to avoid doing what they really need to do, namely, repent of their misdeeds.

The amazing thing is that even though it was very unjust for Adam and Eve to blame God for their sin and misery, God still loved Adam and Eve and sought their salvation. He eventually took the sins of the whole world on himself. He sent his Son, Jesus, to the cross to pay the penalty for our sins. As Paul says, who can grasp how wide and long and high and deep the love of Christ is? His love surpasses knowledge (Ephesians 3:18,19).

The first gospel promise
Adam and Eve had hardly finished accusing God when he graciously announced his plan to save them. As they stood before God, trembling with fear, they probably had a hard time understanding everything God said. But one thing was immediately clear. God was angry with the enemy, who had tricked them and brought about their downfall. That indicated that God still loved them, that he was still their friend.

Even more important, Adam and Eve could not fail to notice that in his words to the serpent, God promised a Savior. He promised a special offspring of the woman, who would crush the serpent's head. From our New Testament vantage point, we realize God was talking about Jesus. Satan would strike Jesus' heel on the cross, and Jesus would die. But at the same time, by taking the world's sins away, Jesus would crush Satan's power over sinners.

Adam and Eve found further comfort in the words God spoke to the serpent: "I will put enmity between you and the woman" (Genesis 3:15). In Hebrew the first word in that sentence is *enmity*, which puts emphasis on that word. In other words, God was saying, "*Enmity, hatred, hostility* will I establish between you, Satan, and the woman."

But wasn't there enough hatred in the world already? Think of the enmity man had shown toward God when he ate the forbidden fruit. Think of the enmity Adam had shown toward his wife when he tried to shift the blame to her. Of course there was enough enmity in the world already. The problem was, all that enmity was misdirected! Man had been foolish in directing his hatred against God and his fellow human being. He didn't know who his friends were! But God promised to teach man what he needed to know. God would change man's heart, bring him to repentance, and show him who his friends and enemies really were. God would have to do this for man because man could never do it for himself.

What is sin?

Now that we have reviewed sin's tragic entry into the world, with all its terrible consequences, we can only conclude that sin is our enemy. Every one of us is engaged in a fierce battle, a deadly war against this enemy. In any war it is good to know the nature and capabilities of the enemy. Therefore it would be good for us to take a closer look at sin so that we might better understand it.

The Bible gives a very simple definition of sin: "Everyone who sins breaks the law; in fact, sin is lawlessness" (1 John 3:4). When Adam and Eve ate the forbidden fruit, they broke God's law. That was sin. They deviated from God's law. They failed to live up to the standard of perfection God had set for them.

When the Bible says "sin is lawlessness," it means that sin is not just a negative concept, in the sense of something missing, expressing a person's lack of perfection, but that sin is also a positive concept, in the sense that something evil is present, that sin is an active opposition to God's holy law. (The use of the term *positive* is not intended to suggest that sin is in any way good.) In other words, in God's view sin is not merely neutral but something actively opposed to him and his law. Sins are not just thoughts, words, and actions that float around innocently in some gray area between right and wrong but vicious attacks on God's sovereignty and holiness.

What is the law?

The command to abstain from the fruit of the tree of the knowledge of good and evil was not the only command God gave man in the garden. When God created man in his image, he inscribed the knowledge of his will in man's heart. Adam and Eve instinctively knew the difference between right and wrong. The Lutheran Confessions state, "Our first parents even before the fall did not live without the law, for the law of God was written into their hearts when they were created in the image of God."[17]

The Lutheran Confessions, furthermore, give an excellent, scriptural definition of the law: "The law is a divine
doctrine which reveals the righteousness and immutable
will of God, shows how man ought to be disposed in his
nature, thoughts, words, and deeds in order to be pleasing
and acceptable to God, and threatens the transgressors of
the law with God's wrath and temporal and eternal punishment."[18] Another commonly used definition of the law
is that the law is God's pronouncement of what we are to
do and not to do and how we are to be, namely, perfect.

When man's perfect knowledge of the law became
obscured by the fall, man still had some knowledge of the
law remaining, witnessed by the voice of his conscience.
This is called natural law. But because the natural law God
wrote into man's heart at creation was not as clear as it
once was, God gave man his law a second time, this time
in written form. He gave a summary of the written law,
called the Ten Commandments, to the Israelites on two
tables of stone on Mount Sinai. For us who live after
Christ, God has repeated the basic content of the Ten
Commandments in the New Testament.

God is the only lawgiver

It is important to remember that the law to which man
is subject is defined and established only by God. The
Bible says there is only one ultimate lawgiver and judge,
God (James 4:12). When the religious leaders of Jesus' day
added their own commandments to the law of God, Jesus
told them they were worshiping God in vain (Matthew
15:9). No one has the right to add or to subtract from
God's law (Revelation 22:18,19). Only God and those
authorities whom God sanctions, such as the government
(Romans 13:1-7) and parents (Colossians 3:20), have the

power to establish what is right and wrong. And God sanctions only those laws of government and other earthly authorities that do not contradict his divine law found in the Bible (Acts 5:29).

In summary, the question of whether or not something is a sin is not determined by what people think or how they feel but by the laws God has given. Just as the views and opinions of men cannot make what is not a sin to be sin, so no one can make something God has pronounced sinful to be righteous.

Go to the source!

In 1888 in Jacksonville, Florida, there was an epidemic of yellow fever, and almost five hundred people died. At that time people didn't know that yellow fever was carried by mosquitoes. They thought it was carried by germs in the air. In order to fight the disease, the army brought in artillery and tried to blast the germs in the air. At the post office, the letters leaving Jacksonville were spread out on the floor and pounded with clubs to kill the germs that might be on them. It was all in vain. If the people of Jacksonville had gotten rid of their mosquitoes, they would have gotten rid of the yellow fever. But they didn't know the source of their problem.

When people look at all the terrible problems that exist in the world today—war in one part, persecution and famines in another, murders and assaults everywhere else—they search for answers. Generally, people feel that man has to look to himself to solve these problems, either by more effort, more education, or more financial sacrifice. Hardly anyone looks to God for help, because God is perceived to be part of the problem. What's the matter with God anyway? Why does he let bad things happen? To many people,

God is the problem, and people are the answer. But to come to that conclusion is just as foolish as thinking you can get rid of yellow fever by bringing in artillery.

When a deadly fire has broken out and caused death and destruction, an arson investigation team seeks to determine the cause of the fire. Is there an odor of gasoline or evidence of an incendiary device to indicate that the fire was set? Or did the fire start near some faulty electrical wiring? To find the cause of the fire, investigators must find out where and how the fire began.

That is what we have done in this chapter. We have traced the fire of sin back to its cause. We have found that it is not God who should be blamed but Satan, who led man into sin. And man himself is also to be blamed, because he had no excuse for doubting God's goodness and accepting Satan's word rather than God's. In subsequent chapters, as we continue to investigate even more thoroughly the fire of sin and its devastating effects on mankind, we will need to keep in mind who struck the match that set man's house aflame.

6

Man's House Is All Aflame

Fire can be both good and bad. A good fire is controlled, confined, and unable to harm the people and property around it. But even a good fire resists confinement and can be dangerous if it escapes. The door of a wood-burning furnace may not be left open, lest sparks fly out and land on something that could ignite. Care must be taken so that fire does not escape.

The great tragedy of Adam and Eve's fall into sin is that from the very start it was a wildfire that immediately spread to all its surroundings. The fall affected not only Adam and Eve but every human being who would live after them. The fire of sin was not confined to a single room, a fire that could be fought or controlled, but it spread everywhere at once. Man's house was all aflame.

Everyone subject to death

Paul describes the effect Adam's sin had on all mankind: "Sin entered the world through one man, and death through sin, and in this way *death came to all men,* because all sinned" (Romans 5:12). This momentous statement tells us that through Adam's fall the entire human race inherited the corruption of sin and became subject to death. In other words, the fall into sin is not just Adam's sin; it is everyone's sin. Because of it, all of us have merited death as a punishment from God.

In case anyone might wonder whether Paul really meant *everyone* was affected by Adam's fall, Paul went on to say, "Death reigned . . . even over those who did not sin by breaking a command, as did Adam" (Romans 5:14). Not just Adam and Eve or those who sinned as they did by breaking a command became subject to death. Through Adam's fall *all* people became subject to death.

From this it is evident that there must be another kind of sin besides actual sin (breaking a command). If all people are sinners and subject to death, as Paul says—even those who have not committed an actual sin—then there must be a kind of sin charged to man other than actual sin. In this way Paul compels us to acknowledge the existence of what theologians call original sin.

Only one exception to original sin

But is it really true that all people are sinners? Even little babies? Even the unborn? David answers yes! He tells us that the guilt of original sin is ours already before we are born. He says, "Surely I was sinful at birth, sinful from the time my mother conceived me" (Psalm 51:5). David was sinful from the first moment of his existence, from his conception. And not just David! *All people,* born or unborn, are sinners before God. The Bible says, "No one living is righteous before you [God]" (Psalm 143:2). "There is no difference, for all have sinned and fall short of the glory of God" (Romans 3:22,23). "The Scripture declares that the whole world is a prisoner of sin" (Galatians 3:22).

The Roman Catholic Church would like to make Mary an exception to the universal problem of original sin. On December 8, 1854, Pope Pius IX proclaimed that Mary's soul, "in the first instant of its creation . . . was, by a special grace and privilege of God, . . . preserved free from all stain of original sin."[19] Roman Catholics have been celebrating the Feast of the Immaculate Conception in Mary's honor on December 8 ever since. Their teaching claims that Mary was free of sin and without need of a Savior. However, Mary herself admitted she had the problem of sin when she called God *her Savior* (Luke 1:46,47).

There was only one immaculate conception, the conception of Mary's son, Jesus Christ. He was immaculately conceived by the Holy Spirit. Since he was conceived in a supernatural way, without a human father, Jesus was not guilty of original sin. Nor was he guilty of actual sin. The Bible says he was "tempted in every way, just as we are—yet was without sin" (Hebrews 4:15). Not even 40 days of intense temptation by the devil in the desert could produce a crack in the armor of his innocence (Luke 4:1-13). When Jesus challenged his enemies to prove him guilty of sin, they couldn't respond directly to his question (John 8:46).

How original sin is passed on

We have seen that Adam was created in God's image to be perfectly holy and righteous (Genesis 1:27). We have also traced the loss of Adam's innocence to his fall into sin

(Genesis 3:1-8). With that background, it is significant that when the Bible reports the arrival of Adam's off-spring, it does not say Adam had children who were made in God's image but, rather, that he "had a son in his own likeness, in his own image" (Genesis 5:3). This can only mean that when Adam fathered children, they bore their sinful father's image rather than God's.

This agrees with what Jesus told Nicodemus: "Flesh gives birth to flesh, but the Spirit gives birth to spirit" (John 3:6). Flesh gives birth to flesh. Sinners give birth to sinners. The sinful flesh we have, our corrupt, sinful nature, which bars us from entering the kingdom of God, comes from the sinful flesh of our parents. The problem is the sinful and corrupted seed from which we are formed. Thus it is clear that original sin is passed on through reproduction. The Lutheran Confessions therefore state, "Original sin is transmitted through our carnal conception and birth out of sinful seed from our father and mother."[20]

Some people believe that the human nature we inherit from our parents is pure, or neutral. They believe that infants are born with a capacity for good and evil and become good or bad when they imitate the people around them. But Paul's words to the Ephesians do not allow such confidence in man's goodness: "We were *by nature* objects of wrath" (2:3). We incur God's anger not because we imitate the bad example of our parents and others, but because of the sinful nature we have at birth.

Original sin: How serious is it?

The biblical evidence makes it impossible to believe that man is inherently good. After the flood God gave a very pessimistic assessment of man's spiritual powers. At a time when only believing Noah and his family were living on the earth, God said that *every* inclination of man's heart is evil from childhood (Genesis 8:21). The apostle Paul admitted the utter lack of spiritual power in the nature he inherited from Adam: "I know that nothing good lives in me, that is, in my sinful nature. For I have the desire to do what is good, but I cannot carry it out" (Romans 7:18).

The Bible describes the corruption of man's nature as *spiritual blindness*. Man's understanding of God's will is darkened (Ephesians 4:18). Man cannot accept the spiritual truths that come from the Spirit of God, because they are foolishness to him (1 Corinthians 2:14). With the nature he has inherited from Adam, man is also *spiritually dead* (Ephesians 2:1). He has no power to bring himself to spiritual life. Worst of all, because of original sin, man is *God's enemy*. Paul says, "The sinful mind is hostile to God" (Romans 8:7). Since man's corrupted nature makes him spiritually blind, dead, and God's enemy, he cannot bring himself into a right relationship with God, nor does he even want to. Original sin is serious indeed!

Original sin: a definition

One of the Lutheran Confessions, the Formula of Concord, defines original sin in this way:

> Original sin is the complete lack or absence of the . . . image of God according to which man was originally created in truth, holiness, and righteousness, together with a disability and ineptitude as far as the things of God are concerned. . . . Original sin in human nature is not only a total lack of good in spiritual, divine things, but . . . at the same time it replaces the lost image of God in man with a deep, wicked, abominable, bottomless, inscrutable, and inexpressible corruption of his entire nature in all its

> powers. . . . By nature every one of us inherits from Adam
> a heart, sensation, and mind-set which, in its highest
> powers and the light of reason, is by nature diametrically
> opposed to God and his highest commands and is actu-
> ally enmity against God, especially in divine and spiritual
> matters. . . . The punishment and penalty of original sin
> which God imposes upon Adam's children and upon
> original sin is death, eternal damnation.[21]

Notice that original sin is described not only in negative terms, as an absence of God's image and a total lack of
good in spiritual things, but also in positive terms, as an
evil that is present, a mind-set that is diametrically
opposed to God. The total depravity and spiritual helplessness that is ours because of original sin is emphasized
through a heaping of terms: "disability," "ineptitude,"
"abominable . . . bottomless corruption." The universality
and the source of original sin are declared: "Every one of
us inherits from Adam . . ." The guilt and punishment that
are ours because of original sin are clearly set forth as
"death" and "eternal damnation."

Is God fair?

Many people object to the doctrine of original sin from
the viewpoint of fairness. They ask how one person's sin
can be charged to the whole human race. Surely, they say,
people should be charged only with the evil deeds they
themselves commit. But God's justice is not determined
by our ideas of fairness. The question ought not be,
"What is fair?" but "What does the Bible teach?" The
Bible teaches the doctrine of original sin so clearly that it
cannot be denied.

The Bible puts this issue of fairness in a proper light
when it makes a connection between the fact that God

charged Adam's sin to all people and the fact that God charged Christ's righteousness to all people. Paul says, "Just as the result of one trespass was condemnation for all men, so also the result of one act of righteousness was justification that brings life for all men" (Romans 5:18). Those who accuse God of being unfair should be consistent. When they reject as unfair the fact that God charged Adam's sin to all people, they also must reject as unfair the fact that God has credited Christ's righteousness to all people. Such a position, however, as Lutheran theologian Francis Pieper says, puts them "outside the pale of Christianity."[22]

Pelagius

At the beginning of the fifth century, a British monk named Pelagius was disturbed by the fact that many Christians in his day seemed to make the doctrines of free grace and original sin a license for sinning. They felt that if they sinned, they could always go to God for forgiveness. God's grace was boundless, so why not sin as much as they could? In the doctrine of original sin, they found a ready excuse, even for the worst of their sins. They could always say: "Sorry, but I can't help it. This is the way I am."

Offended by this, Pelagius began to teach that man's nature was not at all tainted by sin since Adam's fall. Pelagius maintained that Adam's sin had affected only himself and not his offspring. Man's nature was still in its original state, which Pelagius considered morally neutral. According to Pelagius, man was by nature without virtue or vice, but capable of both. His free will was unimpaired by the fall. Man could choose good or evil by his own power and wisdom. God's grace was not needed for man's salvation. Man was perfectly capable of saving himself.

When the church father Augustine exposed Pelagius' teachings as a denial of the truth, others, called semi-Pelagians, began to teach that man's free will was only partially impaired by the fall. They said man's salvation depended on God's grace *and* on the right use of man's natural wisdom and powers. The views of both Pelagius and the semi-Pelagians were rejected by the church at various councils, among them Carthage in 416, Ephesus in 431, and Orange in 529. In spite of such official condemnations, these false teachings continue to be a problem in the Christian church even today, a matter we will discuss further in Chapter 8.

The Flacian controversy

Matthias Flacius (1520–1575) was a leading theologian in the Lutheran church in Germany after the death of Luther. When various controversies arose, Flacius usually could be counted on to defend the truth, even at great cost to himself. He was especially active in defending against the semi-Pelagians, who said man was able to help with his salvation because his spiritual powers were not entirely removed by the fall.

Although Flacius was generally on the side of truth, in a theological debate with a man named Strigel in 1560, Flacius went too far in one of his statements. He identified original sin with the very essence of man's nature. Instead of understanding original sin to be the corrupt quality and condition of soul and body brought upon mankind by Adam's fall, Flacius proclaimed that original sin was human nature itself. Unfortunately, when other Lutherans pointed out the error to Flacius, he refused to take back what he had said.

What Flacius failed to see is that his position made God the creator of sin. As the Formula of Concord points out, "God not only created the body and soul of Adam and Eve before the fall, but also our bodies and souls after the fall."[23] Since God is the creator of man's nature still today, that nature cannot be identical with original sin. Otherwise God is the creator of evil.

Moreover, Flacius' position called into question whether Jesus could be our true brother in the flesh. If our human nature is sin itself, how could Jesus share in our human nature and still be sinless? And if original sin and our human nature are identical, how could God restore our present bodies in the resurrection, as the Bible says he will (Job 19:26,27)? In that case, God would resurrect sin.

For these reasons the Formula of Concord states that a distinction must be made between man's nature and original sin. Original sin is not human nature itself, but only a corruption of human nature. At the same time, it is "so deep a corruption that nothing sound . . . has survived in man's body or soul, in his inward or outward powers."[24]

The chief sin

Since original sin is not a sin we commit, as theft or murder are committed, some have failed to see how it can condemn us. And since original sin cannot be seen, it is difficult for human reason to believe that it exists. But original sin is just as real, just as condemning as any sin we commit. In fact, original sin is really "the chief sin, the root and fountain of all actual sin."[25] It is the driving force within us that leads us into actual sins. Actual sins are the symptoms. Original sin is the disease itself (Matthew 15:19).

We too were lost

Why is it important to remember this? Because it is so easy for us to be self-righteous and to think we are better than others. When we see the terrible actual sins others commit, we may begin to think of sin as a fire burning in someone else's house but not in ours. There is always some sin we haven't committed. We may not have had an abortion. We may never have committed adultery. We may never have engaged in witchcraft or worshiped the devil. And even if we did sin here or there, our sins were different somehow. We had reasons for what we did. God understood, or he looked the other way. God overlooked the bad things we did because he knew that basically we were good. This is the kind of self-righteous thinking we may be tempted to indulge in at times.

If, however, we understand the doctrine of original sin correctly, we realize that in God's eyes none of us are better than others. Like everybody else, we were born lost and condemned, corrupt and depraved, spiritually blind, dead, and God's enemies. Original sin throws every one of us into the same category, the category of those who cannot do one good thing to earn God's favor. With our sinful nature, we can only arouse God's anger. We are all dry tinder in the same vile trash barrel, awaiting the same eternal fire.

Our need for Christ and Baptism

Unless we know and believe this, we will never fully understand our need for Christ as our Savior. He is our only hope. If he had not saved us through his perfect life and his innocent sufferings and death on the cross, we would certainly have been eternally lost. But because of him, God has forgiven and forgotten our sins. God has cast all our sins, including our original sin, into the depths of the ocean (Micah 7:19), where he will never go to look at them again. Through Christ mankind has been reclaimed from the fires of hell.

A proper understanding of original sin not only helps us comprehend the importance of Christ but also the importance of Baptism. Babies are not pure and holy when they are born but in dire need of a new spiritual birth because of original sin. "No one can see the kingdom of God unless he is born again" (John 3:3). But through Baptism, by being "born of water and the Spirit" (verse 5), our little ones receive the new birth they need. They are brought to faith and into God's kingdom. May we never delay bringing them to Jesus in this way!

A mind of his own

Every generation has its science fiction tale of some creation of man that runs amok. Think of Frankenstein, that fictional creation of man who developed a mind of his own and turned into a horrible, murdering monster. In more recent times, Stephen King's automobile Christine developed a mind of its own and began to kill people by locking them inside or running them down.

In real life man is God's creature run amok. God created man for his own glory and to be a creature on whom he could lavish his love. Man was created to live in fellowship with God. He was to live a perfect and righteous life according to the will of God. But then man fell into sin. He developed a mind of his own. Instead of living for God, he began to live for himself.

Instead of God being the center of his world, man places himself at the center. Man lives with one overriding purpose, that he himself be happy. Whatever pleases him is good; whatever displeases him is evil. What God wants may be ignored, and what others need may be overlooked. Only what man wants and needs for himself is indispensable. In this way man has become his own god, instead of letting God be God.

This is the tragic result of original sin. We see it already one generation after Adam and Eve, with Cain killing his brother Abel in a fit of jealousy (Genesis 4:8). We see it today in man's inhumanity to man: not only in the wars and strife going on in far away countries but right in our own homes, between family members. We see it also in ourselves. What we do is not the good we want to do but, rather, the evil we do not want to do (Romans 7:19). No matter where we look, whether at others or ourselves, we see ample evidence of original sin. Man's house—our house—is all aflame.

7

The Fire Shows Itself

A fire burning inside a house is not always apparent at first. A small fire may have started in a wall because of an electrical short. A cigarette may be smoldering on the couch. Or spontaneous combustion may have occurred in a pile of oily rags out in the attached garage. Yet someone walking past that house will not be aware of what is going on inside. Only when the fire shows itself at a window or burns through the roof will a passerby realize the problem. By that time every occupant of the house may already be dead from smoke inhalation.

Original sin, which we discussed in Chapter 6, is the destructive fire inside man's spiritual house that has killed all of us. Though original sin itself cannot be seen, it leads to actual sins, which in many cases can be seen. Original sin is a sinful condition; actual sins are the deeds that result from that sinful condition. The Bible says, "Out of the heart come evil thoughts, murder, adultery, sexual immorality, theft, false testimony, slander" (Matthew 15:19). Actual sins, such as those just listed, demonstrate the existence and power of original sin.

A multitude of transgressions

In this chapter we will focus our attention on the various kinds of actual sin, which demonstrate the existence of inner sin. Just as there are various kinds of fire—wood fires, chemical fires, oil fires, rubber fires, grease fires, electrical fires, nuclear fires, and so on—so there are many different kinds of actual sin. And just as every kind of fire can kill, so all kinds of actual sin are deadly..

In some ways this chapter may be rather depressing. The subject matter is not conducive to a light and happy heart. One kind of sin after another will be described. Like a bell tolling man's death, the names and descriptions of various sins will ring out. What is the purpose for listing and describing all these sins? What can we learn? In this way Scripture impresses upon us the multitude of temptations that confront us and the magnitude of our transgressions. With all these deadly sins paraded before us, we will have a much better understanding of the infinite value of the redemption our Savior earned for us when he died on the cross.

Actual sin: a definition

We have already defined original sin as a sinful condition and actual sin as the deeds resulting from that sinful condition. Use of the term *actual sin* does not suggest that this kind of sin is the only real and true sin. We have seen that the other major kind of sin, original sin, is certainly real and dangerous enough. Actual sins are *actual* only because we act them out or do them.

Actual sin is every act in thought, word, or deed that conflicts with God's will. It may be an act done in violation of one of God's Ten Commandments or an act that conflicts with a special, one-time command of God. God's command to Adam and Eve not to eat of the forbidden fruit was a one-time command that does not apply to us today. God's command to Abraham to sacrifice his son Isaac is another example of a special, one-time command of God.

Whether or not something is a sin is not determined by what we think or how we feel about it but by the word and commands of God. To us, eating fruit may seem to be a rather innocent activity, but it was a sin for Adam and Eve to eat the fruit of that special tree in the Garden of Eden, because God had forbidden it (Genesis 2:17). When the Israelites borrowed silver and gold from the Egyptians with no intent of returning those things (Exodus 12:35,36), we might call that stealing. But it was not a sin for the Israelites to take those things, because God had expressly commanded them to do it (3:22). Today God does not speak to us directly, giving special, one-time commands. Therefore, whether or not something is a sin must be determined from God's holy law as it is recorded in the Scriptures.

People today are very jealous of what they perceive as their rights. Many claim "rights" they do not have. Some claim the right to have an abortion. Others insist on the right to love some people and hate others. However, no one has the right to do anything God has forbidden. Doing what God prohibits in his Word is a sin of commission.

God's commandments are a unit

A common mistake people make is to shorten God's list of Ten Commandments. They treat the Ten Command-ments like a menu in a restaurant, as if they can pick and choose what they want to obey. They feel that if they do not kill or steal, they have attained a level of perfection satisfactory to God. They do not consider their sins of gos-siping or coveting to be as damning as the murder and theft other people may commit. However, God condemns all sins committed against any of his commandments as equally shameful and objectionable.

In fact, God treats the Ten Commandments as a unit. In God's mind a person sinning against one commandment is sinning against all of them. The Bible says, "Whoever keeps the whole law and yet stumbles at just one point is guilty of breaking all of it" (James 2:10). The law works on what we might call the balloon principle: one hole and it is broken forever. Or we could compare the law to a nylon stocking: one run and it is ruined. Or the law is like musical harmony: if just one voice is wrong, the entire harmony is wrong. Again, the law is like a glass window: you may hit it in only one place, but it is shattered all the way through. In terms of the Fifth Commandment, if we love all people and hate only one, in God's eyes it's as if we hated everyone!

Sins of commission and omission

Actual sins are divided into two kinds: sins of commis-sion and sins of omission. Sins of commission are sins committed when we do what God's law forbids us to do. Sins of omission are charged to us when we fail to do what God has commanded. For example, when David commit-ted adultery with Bathsheba (2 Samuel 11:4), he did something God had forbidden. His sin was a sin of commission. When Jonah failed to go and preach to Nineveh after God had commanded him to go, he was guilty of a sin of omission (Jonah 1:1-3).

The sinful character of sins of omission

The Bible stresses the sinful character of sins of omission because we can easily forget that these sins are just as shameful and deadly as sins of commission. In the parable of the talents (Matthew 25:14-30), the man who failed to invest his master's money is called a "wicked, lazy servant" (verse 26). His master (God) commanded him to be thrown "into the darkness, where there will be weeping and gnashing of teeth" (verse 30).

In the same chapter of Matthew, Jesus pictures unbelievers at the last judgment as people who have committed many sins of omission (25:31-46). The King was hungry, and they gave him nothing to eat. He was thirsty, and they gave him nothing to drink. He was a stranger, and they did not invite him in. Therefore "they will go away to eternal punishment, but the righteous to eternal life" (verse 46). We may think this is a harsh verdict, but God gives us gifts and talents for the express purpose of helping others. If we fail to use them for that purpose, we are guilty of sins of omission.

The Mafia has an unwritten but strictly enforced rule that no one fingers a fellow gangster. The penalty for doing so is death. By not telling on his fellow evildoers, the criminal may escape punishment from his fellow men, but his silence is a sin of omission, and God's penalty for sin is eternal death. Jesus' warning is appropriate: "Do not be afraid of those who kill the body but cannot kill the soul. Rather, be afraid of the One who can destroy both soul and body in hell" (Matthew 10:28).

Many young people today seem to be caught up in the same code of silence. Young people detest those who tell on their peers. If a classroom is vandalized or a teacher's grade book is stolen, most of the students in the school may know who the guilty parties are. But no one wants to be an informant. Young people need to be taught that such sins of omission are just as deadly as sins of commission. It is possible to transgress all God's commandments and incur his anger simply by sitting back and doing nothing: "Anyone, then, who knows the good he ought to do and doesn't do it, sins" (James 4:17).

Voluntary and involuntary sins

The apostle Paul spoke of doing evil he didn't want to do (Romans 7:15-20). Peter told the Jews that they and their leaders had acted in ignorance when they killed Jesus, the author of life (Acts 3:15-17). The Old Testament speaks of sins committed unintentionally (Leviticus 4:2,13; Numbers 15:27) and sins committed defiantly (Numbers 15:30). These passages and others like them have led theologians to distinguish between voluntary and involuntary sins.

Voluntary sins are sins committed deliberately and willfully against the dictates of a person's conscience. Such sins cannot live in a person alongside true faith. Voluntary, or willful, sins by believers drive out the Holy Spirit and destroy faith. Involuntary sins are sins committed out of ignorance or weakness. All such sins are serious, but when believers in Jesus commit involuntary sins, such sins do not destroy faith. Judas' betrayal of Jesus is an example of deliberate, premeditated, voluntary sin. Judas made a conscious choice to commit that sin, and the participation of his will can be seen from the considerable amount of planning he did before committing it (Matthew 26:14-16).

Young children and infants are generally considered guilty of involuntary rather than voluntary sins. Though their emotions and wills are sinful and the acts they commit are truly sin, their sins are not committed with the kind of premeditation and mature knowledge adults have. The Bible describes young children and infants as not knowing good from bad (Deuteronomy 1:39).

The sin the Roman soldiers committed by crucifying Jesus is an example of involuntary sin. Recall Jesus' prayer for them on the cross: "Father, forgive them, *for they do not know what they are doing*" (Luke 23:34). Their sin was a sin of ignorance. They were not consciously disobeying God. In their minds they were simply following the orders of their superiors.

This is not to suggest that the sin the Roman soldiers committed was a small or trivial sin. In Revelation John says every eye will see Jesus when he arrives at his second coming, "even those who pierced him" (Revelation 1:7). The fact that the soldiers receive special mention in that verse in no way commends them for what they did. In fact, it shines a spotlight on the shamefulness of their deed. It tells us they especially will mourn Jesus' arrival and be ashamed on judgment day because then they will realize how terrible their sin was.

When the Bible distinguishes between voluntary and involuntary sins, the purpose is not to show that involuntary sins aren't as bad as voluntary sins. Rather, the purpose is to affirm the terrible guilt and shame connected with involuntary sin and then to demonstrate how much more malicious and inexcusable voluntary sin is. No sin committed against God is small! We may think in terms of small and great sins, but we would do better to think in terms of great and greater sins (Luke 12:47,48). Edward Koehler correctly states, "Every sin, however small it may appear to us, is an offense against the majesty of God, and its guilt must be measured by the exalted position of God, against whom it is committed."[26]

Mortal and venial sins

The Roman Catholic Church teaches that certain sins, called mortal sins, by their very nature merit eternal death. To be a mortal sin, the deed must be seriously wrong, the person who does the act must be aware that it is a serious evil, and the person must deliberately want to do this thing which he knows is gravely sinful.[27]

Venial sins, according to the Roman Catholic Church, do not merit death. They are considered minor, or ordinary, sins. They are committed when a person transgresses a divine law that is not grave (very serious) or when a person transgresses God's law without being aware of the seriousness of his actions.[28] The theft of a widow's life savings by someone who knows it is terribly wrong to do that would be a mortal sin. The theft of a penny, an idle word, or a little joke at someone else's expense might be considered a venial sin.

The problem with this distinction is that it gives people the impression that some sins are of little significance before God. But as we pointed out in our discussion of voluntary and involuntary sins, there is no such thing as a small sin committed against God. God does not take any sin lightly! The Bible says, "Cursed is everyone who does not continue to do *everything* written in the Book of the Law" (Galatians 3:10). Jesus said, "I tell you the truth, until heaven and earth disappear, not the smallest letter, not the least stroke of a pen, will by any means disappear from the Law until everything is accomplished" (Matthew 5:18).

It is scriptural, however, to distinguish between mortal and venial sins *in regard to their effect*, in which case we may say all sins are potentially mortal, for "the wages of sin is death" (Romans 6:23). But the moment God sends his Holy Spirit into our hearts and brings us to faith in Jesus as our Savior, our sins become venial. They can no longer destroy us because they are forgiven.

Therefore, whether a sin is mortal or venial depends on the spiritual state of the one who has sinned. All sins committed by an unbeliever are mortal sins because they lead to death (Romans 8:13). The sins of a believer are venial (verses 1,31-34), unless they drive faith from the believer's heart and fail to result in repentance.

The unforgivable sin

One sin, however, by its very nature, is unforgivable, the so-called sin against the Holy Spirit. Jesus spoke of this sin: "I tell you, every sin and blasphemy will be forgiven men, but the blasphemy against the Spirit will not be forgiven" (Matthew 12:31). The context in which Jesus spoke these words helps us understand what the unforgivable sin is. A blind and mute man possessed by a demon had been brought to Jesus, and Jesus had healed him. The people were astonished and began to wonder if Jesus might be the promised Messiah. Through this miracle the Holy Spirit was working mightily to convince everyone that Jesus was the Savior.

The Pharisees themselves may have been convinced that this miracle was performed by God, but they stubbornly refused to yield to the working of the Holy Spirit. Hoping to counteract the impression this miracle had made on themselves and others, they said, "It is only by Beelzebub, the prince of demons, that this fellow drives out demons" (Matthew 12:24). To call the work of the Holy Spirit the work of the devil was a horrible blasphemy! In this connection Jesus warned the Pharisees against the unforgivable sin. To blaspheme against the Holy Spirit, to maliciously and stubbornly attack his testimony, is a key element of the unforgivable sin.

Hebrews 6:4-6 and 10:26 help round out the biblical description of the unforgivable sin. We learn that this is a sin committed by "those who have once been enlightened" (6:4) and those who "have received the knowledge of the truth" (10:26). Yet they "deliberately keep on sinning" (10:26) and "fall away" (6:6). From all that has been said, it is apparent that the unforgivable sin consists of three elements: (1) a deliberate and stubborn rejection of the gospel, (2) against one's better knowledge, and (3) accompanied by a blasphemous and malicious attack against the gospel.

Who commits this sin?

Sometimes the false idea is suggested that the unforgivable sin is unbelief. The reasoning goes like this: All unbelievers go to hell, and thus all unbelievers are unforgiven. Therefore, unbelief is the unforgivable sin.

However, we must be careful not to charge every unbeliever with the unforgivable sin. First of all, the Bible does not charge all unbelievers with this sin. Second, the Bible distinguishes between unbelievers and those guilty of the unforgivable sin when it instructs us to pray for all people in general, including unbelievers (1 Timothy 2:1), but not for those who are guilty of "a sin that leads to death" (1 John 5:16). Third, every unbeliever who comes to faith is proof that not all unbelievers have committed the unforgivable sin. Finally, recall the threefold scriptural definition of the unforgivable sin, given earlier. Though all unbelievers reject the gospel, there is no evidence to conclude they all do so blasphemously or against better knowledge.

Similarly, we should not assume all blasphemers have committed the unforgivable sin. Before the apostle Paul came to faith, he was a blasphemer who viciously attacked the work of the Holy Spirit. Yet he did not commit the unforgivable sin, because he acted in ignorance (1 Timothy 1:13). Nor are all those who fall from faith or who deny the truth guilty of this sin. Peter denied Jesus publicly and emphatically, but he did so out of fear rather than malice and hatred.

Many times when people hear there is an unforgivable sin, they worry they may have committed it. But their concern is evidence that they have not committed it. Anyone who worries about his sins and has a heartfelt longing not to be excluded from God's love and forgiveness has the Holy Spirit working in him. The Bible says, "It is God who works in you to will and to act according to his good purpose" (Philippians 2:13). God is working in us—we have faith!—when we desire to be saved through Christ.

One last thing about the unforgivable sin: It is not unpardonable because God is unwilling to forgive it. Nor is it a sin for which Christ failed to obtain forgiveness. The merits of Christ are sufficient to atone for all sins (1 John 1:7). The problem is the spiritual condition of the person who has committed the unforgivable sin. His stubborn and malicious rejection against his own better knowledge drives the Holy Spirit from his heart. As a judgment against him, the Holy Spirit leaves him, never to return.

The sin of obduracy

The sin of obduracy is similar in some respects to the unforgivable sin. The sin of obduracy is the sin of persistently and stubbornly hardening oneself by resisting the Word of God and the testimony of conscience. One key difference between the unforgivable sin and the sin of obduracy is that the former is a hardening against the gospel but the latter may be a hardening against either the law or the gospel.

The sin of obduracy is best illustrated in the actions of Pharaoh, who hardened himself against the command of God to let the Israelites go. Repeatedly God demanded that Pharaoh obey him and free the Israelites. Repeatedly Pharaoh refused. Through the first five plagues, Pharaoh hardened his own heart (Exodus 8:15,32), but after the sixth plague, we are told, "The LORD hardened Pharaoh's heart" (9:12).

The sin of obduracy involves a process. First a person repeatedly and persistently rejects what God commands. The person resists God's Word and his conscience is weakened until the person has so sufficiently hardened himself that from force of habit, he has no recourse from the path of destruction. Then God takes notice of this stubborn and persistent disobedience and, as a judgment against it, further hardens the person, who has already hardened himself.

In Romans 1:18-32 Paul describes in detail this process of hardening among the ungodly. They know God, yet neither glorify him as God nor give thanks to him. Their hearts are darkened. Against their better knowledge, they become fools and choose to worship someone or something else. They harden themselves in stubborn disobedience and idolatry. In judgment against them, God then hardens them further and gives them over completely to the service of such sins as greed, envy, homosexuality, murder, strife, slander, and arrogance. Again, we see the standard sequence of events that takes place in the sin of obduracy: first a person hardens himself; only then does God harden him further.

Both Pharaoh and the evildoers Paul condemned in Romans 1:18-32 hardened themselves against the law. God's Old Testament people (Isaiah 6:9-11) and the Jews who rejected Jesus (Matthew 13:14) hardened themselves against the gospel. They persistently despised the good news of their salvation. They blocked the light that was trying to penetrate their hearts. They smothered the faint light that was struggling to remain in their hearts. God then decided to darken their hearts even further.

What a warning to us to struggle against the first stirrings of sin in our hearts. Sin cannot be allowed to establish a foothold in our hearts or lives. If sin is allowed to grow, it ultimately can drive out faith itself!

Sins against conscience

The conscience is a voice inside man testifying to the existence of God and his law. When we obey the conscience, it tells us a higher being is pleased with us. When we disobey, it tells us that higher being is angry.

Since Adam's fall into sin, the conscience may not always agree with the Word of God on questions of morality (1 Corinthians 4:4). Sometimes its knowledge may be incomplete (Romans 7:7). Theologians distinguish four types of conscience:

> 1. A correct conscience, one that is correctly informed and agrees with the Word of God

2. An erring or misinformed conscience, one that disagrees with the Word of God

3. A probable conscience, one that has been neglected and is unable to guide a person in his actions because it lacks instruction

4. A doubting conscience, one that is not sure what is right or wrong in a certain matter

A person who acts against a correct conscience commits a grievous sin. In this case the sinner has full knowledge that his actions are prohibited in God's Word. If he repeats and persists in such a sin, it may lead him to the sin of obduracy, discussed earlier, or even to the unforgivable sin.

A person with an erring conscience sins no matter what he does. Consider the example of the heathen who believes he should worship an idol. Such a person sins by following his conscience, because God has forbidden him to worship an idol. However, he also sins if he fails to follow his conscience, because he believes that God wants him to do something but then fails to do it. In this case he violates the divine command to put God first in his life.

A person with a probable conscience, one that has been neglected, has a problem of the heart. Instead of giving his conscience the knowledge and instruction from God's Word that it needs, he has treated important moral matters lightly. We sometimes speak of such a person as having little or no sense of right and wrong. God wants us to be concerned about choosing the right course of action. He wants us to instruct our consciences by a thorough study of his Word. He welcomes our prayers that implore him to help us make right decisions.

A person with a doubting conscience is unsure whether what he proposes to do is morally right or wrong. He has misgivings and apprehensions. In regard to someone who is not sure whether it is right to eat meat or drink wine, Paul says, "The man who has doubts is condemned if he eats, because his eating is not from faith; and everything that does not come from faith is sin" (Romans 14:23). By *faith* Paul means the sure conviction that an act is in accordance with God's will. If a person acts without that conviction, he is demonstrating that he does not feel God's will is important. His lack of concern for God's will condemns him. First we must discover what God's will is, Paul says. Only then should we act, and only in accordance with God's will!

The causes of sin

In Chapter 5 we saw that it was not God's fault that sin entered the world. It was Satan's fault and man's fault as well. Adam and Eve had no excuse when they believed the devil's word instead of God's. God may permit sin to occur, but he does not *cause* sin. God is holy (Leviticus 19:2) and would never design or initiate something sinful.

When the Bible speaks of the causes of sin since the fall of Adam, it speaks of internal and external causes. The internal cause of sin is man's sinful nature, the original sin we inherited from Adam and Eve. Paul calls the sins we commit "acts of the sinful nature" (Galatians 5:19). The external causes are the devil (Ephesians 2:2), other people (1 Corinthians 15:33; 2 Peter 2:1-3), human philosophy (Colossians 2:8), and various things in the world (1 John 2:15-17).

Temptation is when the devil, the world, or the sinful nature try to lure us into sin. The Bible is quick to say God does not tempt us to sin: "When tempted, no one should say, 'God is tempting me.' For God cannot be tempted by evil, nor does he tempt anyone; but each one is tempted when, by his own evil desire, he is dragged away and enticed" (James 1:13,14). God is not responsible for the evil temptations that assail us, but encourages us to pray to him for help against temptation (Matthew 6:13; 26:41) and promises us a way out in temptation (1 Corinthians 10:13).

The sins of offense

Finally, the Bible distinguishes between the sin of *giving* offense and the sin of *taking* offense. To give offense means to lead a person into sin or even into unbelief. The Bible warns us repeatedly not to cause anyone to stumble in his faith (1 Corinthians 10:32; Romans 14:13). Jesus warns us not to give offense especially to children: "If anyone causes one of these little ones who believe in me to sin, it would be better for him to have a large millstone hung around his neck and to be drowned in the depths of the sea" (Matthew 18:6).

Offense can be given not only by false doctrine and sin but also by a careless use of Christian liberty. In the case of the man not sure whether it is right to eat meat or drink wine (Romans 14:14-23; 1 Corinthians 8:4-13), Paul warns repeatedly that no one should lead such a weak brother to sin against his doubting conscience. The rule Paul urges upon us is to relinquish our Christian liberty for the sake of a weak brother unless the truth of the gospel is at stake. Better never to eat meat again than to cause a brother to fall (1 Corinthians 8:13). But if the weak and erring brother insists we follow his error, we must obey Paul's command to stand firm in our freedom (Galatians 5:1).

Taking offense is the sin of finding fault with true doctrine or Christian conduct. Even the sinless Son of God became a stumbling stone to the Jews (Romans 9:32) and foolishness to the Gentiles (1 Corinthians 1:23). We should not be surprised if people take offense at the gospel today or reject the pronouncements of God's law. We ought not expect better treatment than what God himself receives.

Keep on fighting those fires!

Firefighters' work is never done. Training sessions are held regularly to keep them at the top of their fire-fighting capabilities. During times of relative inactivity, the fire station and equipment must be cleaned. Just when the cleaning is done, a call may come in signaling a four-alarm fire. Soot and grime collect on the fire engines at the scene of the fire, so all the equipment must be cleaned and polished when the firemen return. Ask firefighters, and they will tell you their work is never done.

So it is with sin. Even the greatest of the saints in the Bible struggled with sin. Peter was brash and self-confident and had to learn humility. John was a "son of thunder," impatient with those who weren't as perfect as he was, and had to learn love. All the saints had to take up the broom of repentance again and again to sweep sin out of the corners of their lives. Every one of them had to fight the fires of sin that broke out in their lives.

Is there any sin in our lives that needs to be swept out? Is there any fire of sin that needs to be drowned in tears of repentance? Have we harbored some secret grudge against our neighbor? Is there any anger in our hearts? any envy? any discontent? any reluctance to do God's will? Like the firefighters' work, our work against sin is never done.

It is wonderful to know that our gracious God has supplied the permanent answer to the fire of sin in our lives.

"The blood of Jesus, his Son, purifies us from all sin"
(1 John 1:7). In the sufferings and death of his Son, God
finished once and for all the work we could not complete.
He put out the fires of sin that were threatening to send
us directly to the eternal lake of fire (Revelation 20:10).
In response to his continuing mercy and forgiveness, how
could we ever reject him and embrace the deadly fires
of sin?

8

Nothing Left but Ashes

How do you describe someone who is helpless? "Help-less as a kitten" is a common expression, but it doesn't describe the danger the kitten is in. "Helpless as a fly caught in a spider web" is better, because in our mind's eye we can see the spider feeling the fly's struggles on the web and quickly moving over to the fly to wrap it up and suck out its lifeblood. But even a picture like that doesn't stir our emotions, because nobody really cares about flies.

To be really moved by a picture of helplessness, we have to see that helplessness in people. Years ago, helplessness was pictured as a young girl tied to a railroad track with a train coming. Today we might think of infants mistreated by their parents or political prisoners forced to undergo

107

painful medical experiments. There is nothing those people can do to free themselves from their predicament.
They are helpless.

Our tragic spiritual helplessness

But even such examples of helplessness are nothing
compared to the tragic spiritual helplessness that afflicts
all of us as we come into this world. At the moment of
conception, we are captives of Satan (2 Timothy 2:26).
We are bound by the shackles of original sin (Psalm 51:5).
We are locked outside the family of God. We are "without
hope and without God in the world" (Ephesians 2:12).
Without saving faith, we are headed straight for the eternal torture of hell.

Moreover, we are unable to free ourselves from this
predicament. We are spiritually blind, so we cannot see or
understand God's wisdom, even if we wanted to (1 Corinthians 2:14). We are spiritually dead, so we are helpless to
bring ourselves to spiritual life (Ephesians 2:1). And we
are God's enemies, afraid of God and hostile to God, fighting his every attempt to save us (Romans 8:7). Unlike the
fly that struggles to save itself, we struggle against our salvation. Paul emphasizes that none of us enters this world
without this dreadful spiritual condition when he quotes
Psalm 14: "There is no one righteous, not even one; there
is no one who understands, no one who seeks God"
(Romans 3:10,11).

Biblical evidence

The biblical evidence for the spiritual helplessness of
fallen, sinful man is overwhelming. The Bible documents
a complete lack of spiritual power in the human nature. In
Genesis 6:5 God looked down on mankind and concluded

that *every* inclination of the thoughts of man's heart is only evil *all the time*. This passage alone is ample proof of the total depravity of the human nature. How can unconverted, natural man will or do anything good if he is only capable of evil all the time? We could compare the human nature to a pencil on a sloped desk. If left to itself, it can only go in one direction. So too, the human nature inevitably falls into sin.

Consider the words of Jeremiah: "The heart is deceitful above all things and beyond cure. Who can understand it?" (Jeremiah 17:9). The human heart is not spiritually neutral. It is so perverted and desperately wicked that no one can fathom how evil it is! In Matthew 7:18 Jesus says, "A bad tree *cannot* bear good fruit." Those who are without faith and are still in their sins are bad trees. They cannot do anything but sin and bear bad fruit. They have no ability to do anything good. The apostle Paul states, "I know that *nothing good* lives in me, that is, in my sinful nature" (Romans 7:18).

We can only conclude that man by nature is absolutely incapable of doing anything right in a spiritual sense. We are not only *weakened* in our spiritual powers; we are *dead*. The Lutheran Confessions testify to natural man's complete spiritual helplessness: "Scripture denies to the intellect, heart, and will of the natural man every capacity, aptitude, skill, and ability to think anything good or right in spiritual matters, to understand them, to begin them, to will them, to undertake them, to do them, to accomplish or to cooperate in them as of himself."[29]

Erasmus versus Luther

The Dutch humanist Desiderius Erasmus (1466–1536) was perhaps the most respected scholar in Europe at the time of Martin Luther. When Erasmus saw the rift that had developed between Luther and the pope of Rome, he at first tried to maintain his neutrality. At times he would praise both sides for what he considered their correctness, and at other times he would condemn both for what he thought were intemperate attacks on one another. Erasmus enjoyed acting as a judge over the two warring sides, and he fancied himself a peacemaker.

Erasmus received unrelenting pressure from both sides to take a stand on the issues that divided Luther and Rome. Finally, bowing to the pressure from Rome, Erasmus wrote a book, *The Freedom of the Will*, in which he took up his pen against Luther. In his book Erasmus claimed that man's will, in spite of Adam's fall, was free. Man had free choice. He had at least some ability to turn toward or away from that which leads to eternal salvation. In discussing the various opinions people had set forth on the matter of free will in the past, Erasmus said, "I prefer the view of those who do attribute much to free choice, but most to grace."[30]

According to Erasmus, the Bible was unclear as to how much people could contribute to their salvation, but it *seemed* to say that we can will and do *something* good. Erasmus argued that God would not command us in the Bible to do so many things if we, by nature, were unable to do any of them. The purpose of the law was not only to reveal sin but to show what man was capable of doing, if only in part.

In keeping with his cherished role as mediator, Erasmus maintained that his differences with Luther on the matter of free will were not all that important. Since Scripture was unclear and the church fathers seemed to disagree with one another, how could anyone know what the truth was?

Luther's response

Luther countered Erasmus by writing a book called *The Bondage of the Will*. There Luther steadfastly denied that sinful, natural man had any free will to turn toward God in spiritual matters. Luther even described the will of natural man as a "beast of burden": "If God rides it, it wills and goes where God wills. . . . If Satan rides it, it wills and goes where Satan wills; nor can it choose to run to either of the two riders or to seek him out, but the riders themselves contend for the possession and control of it."[31]

While Erasmus appealed primarily to logic and human reasoning, Luther appealed to Scripture. He argued that the Bible was very clear on the matter of free will. With one Bible passage after another, he demonstrated the tragic consequences of original sin and Adam's fall.

Luther did not deny that man has the ability to make good and bad decisions in everyday matters based on reason. He did not deny that man can achieve a form of civil righteousness so that he appears to be a godly person on the outside. But by his free will, man can never attain the righteousness of God. That can only be attained through faith in Christ. Therefore Luther maintained that free will exists only in name. When man's free will does what it can, it commits sin.

Is Christ needed?

More than once Luther used his favorite argument: If Erasmus were right, if man had some natural good within him that would either earn God's grace or influence God to give man his grace, that would make Christ's work much less important—perhaps even unnecessary. What kind of Redeemer would Christ be then? If man were able to redeem even a small part of himself, what need would he have of Christ? And what need would he have of the Holy Spirit? Erasmus' doctrine of the freedom of the will robbed God of at least some of his glory and attributed that glory to man.[32]

This controversy centering on the freedom of the will was one of the most important episodes of the Reformation. It put a bright spotlight on the two most important doctrines of the Bible: the spiritual helplessness of man as taught by God's law and the undeserved mercy of God as revealed by the gospel. Luther himself thanked Erasmus for challenging him on this matter. Erasmus had aimed "at the vital spot," as Luther called it, rather than wearying him with trifles like the papacy or purgatory.[33] Luther was happy to trumpet the difference between his theology and that of his opponents regarding the matter of free will.

Sadly, this same difference between Lutherans and Roman Catholics still exists. A 1965 Roman Catholic publication quotes various councils from the 9th to the 16th centuries and approves of their definition of grace as an ability God gives man to prepare the way for his justification. The publication applauds statements of the councils that said not all the actions of an unbeliever are sinful and agrees with those councils that stated, "Free will is by no means taken away [from natural man], but only weakened and inclined to evil."[34] Sadly, the Roman Catholic Church's position remains the same to this day. In this respect, Erasmus would feel very much at home in the Roman Catholic Church today.

Conversion

A subject closely related to free will is the Bible's teaching on conversion. Does a person have the power to take the first step toward God? Can natural man cooperate with God before or in conversion? Do people have the ability to make a decision for Christ? Some popular modern evangelists like Billy Graham and some institutions like Campus Crusade for Christ would answer yes to those questions. But as we shall see, in taking that position, they are attributing to man a power he does not have.

In the course of historical Christianity, three major views have surfaced to credit man with some role in his conversion:

1. *The Pelagian view:* Man by his own powers, without the help of the Holy Spirit, can turn himself to God, believe the gospel, keep the commandments perfectly, and merit eternal life. Man's nature was not at all corrupted by the fall.

2. *The semi-Pelagian view:* Man and God cooperate in conversion. Man by his own powers can make a beginning of his conversion but cannot complete it without God's grace and assistance.

3. *The synergistic, or Arminian, view:* Man and God cooperate in conversion. Man needs the Holy Spirit to begin his conversion, but then the will of man from its own natural powers helps, if only very slightly, to prepare itself to believe the gospel. Included in this group are those who claim that some men cooperate by resisting the Holy Spirit less than others.

Of the three views briefly outlined, synergism reduces man's cooperation to what some might consider a harmless minimum, but it still denies salvation by grace alone. What difference does it make if man has to make a small or large contribution to his salvation? We let the apostle Paul answer the question for us: "If by grace, then it is no longer by works; if it were, grace would no longer be grace"

(Romans 11:6). If there is any contribution by man, salvation is no longer by grace.

Based on logic

The basis for all three positions comes from logic rather than Scripture. A typical argument is the one Erasmus used in his debate with Luther: God commands us to repent and believe. It would be a cruel mockery to command people to do what one knows they are not able to do. Therefore man must have some ability to help with his conversion.

A fundamental weakness with this logical argument is that it proves too much. If God requires a complete saving faith and man is capable of doing whatever God demands, then man must be able to produce faith all by himself, without God's help. But only the extreme Pelagians claimed that much ability for man.

One cannot simply beg the question and assume man has the ability to effect his own conversion. Edward Koehler's statement on this bears repeating:

> The fact that man is capable of being converted does not prove that he is also able to convert himself or to contribute anything towards his conversion. Iron can be melted, but it cannot melt itself; the dead shall be raised, but they cannot raise themselves; men are converted, but no one has ever converted himself or helped in bringing about his conversion. Conversion is a passive experience.[35]

Conversion: an act of God

In opposition to the various Pelagian views and synergism, the Bible credits conversion entirely to God. This biblical doctrine is called divine monergism (God's work alone).

Already in the Old Testament, Ezekiel declared that God had to give his people believing hearts, or they could not be saved: "I will give you a new heart and put a new spirit in you; I will remove from you your heart of stone and give you a heart of flesh" (Ezekiel 36:26). Luke tells us God opens the minds of people to believe the Scriptures: "He [Jesus] opened their minds so they could understand the Scriptures" (Luke 24:45). John points out that the children of God, those who believe in his name, are "children born not of natural descent, *nor of human decision* or a husband's will, but *born of God*" (John 1:13). Paul writes, "No one can say, 'Jesus is Lord,' except by the Holy Spirit" (1 Corinthians 12:3). Paul calls our salvation a gift (Ephesians 1:6) and makes the distinction that man doesn't *work* for his faith but that God *gives* it: "It is by grace you have been saved, through faith—and this not from yourselves, it is the gift of God—not by works, so that no one can boast" (2:8,9).

Three times in his epistle to the Philippians, Paul ascribes the entire work of conversion to the Holy Spirit: "He who began a good work in you will carry it on to completion until the day of Christ Jesus" (1:6). "It has been *granted* to you on behalf of Christ not only *to believe on him*, but also to suffer for him" (1:29). "*It is God who works in you* to will and to act according to his good purpose" (2:13).

Jeremiah compares the unbeliever to a "bush in the wastelands" (Jeremiah 17:6). A bush can't dig itself up and move from the middle of the desert to a privileged spot along the river. Neither can natural man in his helpless spiritual condition take a step toward God. Centuries later, that is exactly what Jesus told those who refused to believe in him: "No one can come to me unless the Father who sent me draws him" (John 6:44).

Word pictures

Some of the word pictures the Bible uses to describe the work of the Holy Spirit emphasize that our faith is entirely his work. Jesus compares conversion to a birth (John 3:5,6). No one gives birth to himself or causes his own birth. Similarly, no one is able to effect his own rebirth to faith.

The Spirit's work is also called quickening. To *quicken* means to "animate" or to "bring to life." No dead person can bring himself to life. The Bible says that when we were dead in our sins, God made us alive with Christ (Ephesians 2:4,5; Colossians 2:13). Nowhere does the Bible picture natural man as merely spiritually weak or sick. Rather, natural man is completely lacking the smallest spark of spiritual life. When the Holy Spirit begins his work in us, we are all spiritual corpses and would remain so if he did not bring us to life.

The Bible's doctrine of conversion is summed up by Luther in his explanation to the Third Article of the Apostles' Creed: "I believe that I cannot by my own thinking or choosing believe in Jesus Christ, my Lord, or come to him. But the Holy Spirit has called me by the gospel, enlightened me with his gifts, sanctified and kept me in the true faith." Luther believed that none of us chooses God. God chooses us. In fact, God bringing us to faith is no less a miracle than raising the dead.

Who died?

There's a story about a minister who invited his congregation to a funeral but did not tell them who had died. Amazingly, they all came, not knowing whose funeral it was. In the funeral sermon, the minister did not describe the deceased as a good person, but as someone so sinful and corrupt that he was surely at that very moment taking up residence in hell. This was shocking to those who heard the sermon. Even though the minister had often preached about the seriousness of sin, none of them could imagine anyone actually being in hell.

When the sermon was over, the minister announced that it was time for everyone to pay their last respects to the corpse. The casket was opened, and all those in attendance filed by to see who this wicked person was who had died. To their surprise, there was nothing in the casket but a large mirror. Everyone who looked in saw *himself* in the casket!

In this chapter and in previous ones, we, in a spiritual sense, have been looking in a mirror. The picture we have seen is not pretty. We have been told that because of original sin we have "a deep, wicked, abominable, bottomless, inscrutable, and inexpressible corruption" on the inside.[36] We have been told that the dirt and filth of many actual sins is covering us on the outside. The degree of decay and corruption on the inside is unmistakable. Each of us, looking into the mirror of the law, has been looking at a corpse.

Like the congregation that heard that sinners deserve to go to hell but could not imagine anyone, much less themselves, going there, we too have a problem believing how corrupt we are on the inside and how filthy we are on the outside. Unless we see ourselves in the casket, we do not really understand our need for new life in Christ.

Death in the midst of life

Man's life on earth actually begins in a spiritual casket. When Adam and Eve ate of the forbidden fruit, they died, and all mankind died with them. Because of their fall into sin, death is now the spiritual state of all who are born. The wages of both original and actual sin is death (Romans

6:23). Therefore people are born spiritually dead, eventually die a temporal death, and, at the moment of temporal death, enter a state of eternal death. Unless God intervenes, man's life from beginning to end is a state of death.

It may seem contradictory to say man's life is a state of death. But we must understand that death is not annihilation. Even though our dead bodies may be turned to dust, Jesus tells us they are in their graves waiting for the resurrection (John 5:28,29).

Three kinds of death

Death must be understood as separation rather than annihilation. *Spiritual death* is the separation of the soul from God. A person is spiritually dead when he does not trust in God's goodness in Christ, when he has no faith, no personal relationship with God. Thus a person can be physically alive and spiritually dead at the same time. *Temporal death* is the separation of the soul from the body. "The dust returns to the ground it came from, and the spirit returns to God who gave it" (Ecclesiastes 12:7). *Eternal death* is the eternal separation of the soul and body from God. Eternal death takes place when a person in a state of spiritual death suffers temporal death. In hell the person is separated from God's love and mercy and experiences only his wrath and punishment for sin.

Most people already think of death as separation. Death separates people from their loved ones, from their earthly possessions, from a life and world they have come to love. But for the unbeliever, death is all of that and more. For the unbeliever death is separation from God. To be abandoned by God's love for eternity is the worst of all possible fates because God is the only source of all goodness and blessings. When the rich man in Jesus' parable of the rich man and Lazarus is denied one drop of water to cool his tongue, we learn volumes about a place where we do not want to go (Luke 16:19-31). Yet if we are left to ourselves, we could never escape that death.

Only ashes

If you have ever visited the site of a forest fire, you know what desolation is. Everything is black. There is no beauty, no sound, no insects, no birds, no wildlife, no sign of life anywhere. The smell of burnt wood still smoldering offends the senses and prompts the visitor to turn away in disgust. Search everywhere in that burned out forest, and you will not find one ray of hope, not one indication that the forest will live again.

But God has ways of bringing the dead to life. Return to that same forest ten years later, and you will find the forest renewed. New trees have begun to grow. Everything is green. Everywhere there is life, beauty, and hope.

So it is with man. When Adam and Eve lit the match of sin in the Garden of Eden, it produced a fire that burned and destroyed them completely. Before the fall they had been light in the Lord; after it they were darkness (Ephesians 5:8). Before the fall they were beloved children of God; after it they were by nature objects of wrath (2:3). Before the fall they experienced freedom, obedience, and life; after it they experienced slavery, disobedience, and death (2:1). Life and beauty were gone. The fire of sin had completely ravaged mankind. There was nothing left but ashes.

But God found a way to bring the dead to life again. He found a way to bring beauty out of ashes. He did it through his Son, Jesus Christ. That will be the subject of the next chapter.

Part III

Glory Restored

9

God's Glorious Restoration of Man

We live in a society in which many broken things can be fixed. You can have a deep scratch on your car fender fixed at an auto body shop. You can patch a hole in your jeans. You can wash your dirty clothes. You can take Librium or Valium prescribed by your doctor if your nerves are frazzled. Everything seems easy to fix, yes, *almost* everything!

But what do you do about sin? You can't paint over it. You can't patch it. You can't wash it or wish it away. There's nothing more pathetic in the Lenten story than the picture of Pontius Pilate with his hands in a wash basin trying to wash away his guilt. No amount of human effort is going to take away sin. The price God demands for sin is too great for man to pay. The Bible says, "The

ransom for a life is costly, no payment is ever enough"
(Psalm 49:8).

God's promise

But what man is unable to do, God accomplished. After
Adam and Eve fell into sin, God promised that the
woman's offspring would crush the serpent's head (Genesis
3:15). Isaiah spoke of God's Suffering Servant: "despised
and rejected by men . . . pierced for our transgressions . . .
crushed for our iniquities; the punishment that brought us
peace was upon him, and by his wounds we are healed"
(Isaiah 53:3,5).

Other, more general, promises of forgiveness gave God's
Old Testament people hope that somehow, some way God
would forgive them. Through his prophet Isaiah, God said:
"Come now, let us reason together. . . . Though your sins
are like scarlet, they shall be as white as snow; though they
are red as crimson, they shall be like wool" (Isaiah 1:18).
Micah promised that God would hurl all their iniquities
into the depths of the sea (Micah 7:19).

The Day of Atonement

The rituals and sacrifices God commanded the Israelites
to perform gave additional promise that there was forgiveness for sin. Perhaps the most vivid ritual was the annual
Day of Atonement, described in Leviticus 16. On the Day
of Atonement, the high priest made elaborate preparations
before he entered the Most Holy Place. He bathed very
carefully. Then, instead of his ornate priestly robes, he put
on simple, linen garments. To further purify himself, he sacrificed a bull for his own sins and the sins of his family.

Incense thrown on live coals taken from the altar
served as a protection so that he, a sinner, could appear

before the holy God. A goat was sacrificed for the sins of the people, and its blood was taken into the Most Holy Place to be sprinkled on the atonement cover of the ark of the covenant. Then, withdrawing from the Most Holy Place, the high priest bathed once again, changed clothes, and offered more sacrifices: a ram for his own sins and another ram for the sins of the people.

All these elaborate preparations and this shedding of blood emphasized that sin was no small matter. Its removal was not easy. Nevertheless, the rituals and sacrifices assured the Israelites that somehow God would forgive them.

Because someone might still doubt his forgiveness, another goat was set aside on the Day of Atonement, the "scapegoat." The high priest laid both hands on its head and confessed over it in a general way all the sins the Israelites had committed in the past year, all the sins for which they had already sacrificed, all the sins of which they were ignorant, and all the sins they were ashamed to confess to another person. In symbolic fashion the weight and burden of all those sins were lifted off the shoulders of the Israelites and put upon the head of that goat. Then the goat was led far away into the wilderness and released. Abandoned in the desert in the midst of bears, lions, and wolves, it would never return. The sins it carried into the wilderness would be gone forever.

Vicarious atonement

Through the symbolism connected with sacrificial animals slain on the altar and through Isaiah's prophecy of God's Suffering Servant, God encouraged his people to think in terms of a *vicarious*, or *substitutionary*, *atonement*. Someone else would take the people's sins upon himself and suffer their punishment for them. But who would that someone be? Who would step forward to take man's punishment and free him from his burden of guilt once and for all?

God the Father entrusted the task of man's redemption to none other than his only Son, Jesus Christ. The apostle Paul says, "When the time had fully come, God sent his Son, born of a woman, born under law, to redeem those under law, that we might receive the full rights of sons" (Galatians 4:4,5).

Jesus, the unique God-man

Jesus was unique in that he was both divine and human at the same time. He was both God and man. He possessed his divine nature from all eternity, together with the Father and the Holy Spirit. He assumed his human nature when he was conceived and born of the virgin Mary.

Jesus' divine nature can be seen from the divine names given him in the Bible (1 John 5:20), the divine characteristics he had (John 1:1,2), his divine works (verse 3), and the divine honor and glory the Bible says he has (5:23). His human nature can be seen from the fact that he is repeatedly called a man (1 Timothy 2:5; Hebrews 2:14) and ascribed a human body and soul (Luke 24:39; Matthew 26:38) and human feelings and actions (Matthew 4:2; John 11:35).

As a man Jesus was under the law. As God he could fulfill the law (Galatians 4:4,5). As a man he could die. As God his death was a sufficient ransom for the sins of the world (Hebrews 10:11-14). As a man he could take our place in the struggle against our enemies: sin, death, and the devil. As God he could defeat those great enemies (Hebrews 2:14). It certainly took someone unique to carry out God's wonderful plan of salvation.

Universal and objective justification

The sinless life of Jesus Christ, his innocent sufferings and death, and his glorious resurrection were decisive events that reversed the results of Adam's fall into sin. Paul contrasts the disaster Adam brought upon all mankind with the salvation Jesus brought to all: "Just as the result of one trespass was condemnation for all men, so also the result of one act of righteousness was justification that brings life for all men. For just as through the disobedience of the one man the many were made sinners, so also through the obedience of the one man the many will be made righteous" (Romans 5:18,19).

A key phrase in the above passage tells us that Jesus' act of righteousness results in "justification that brings life for all men." No one is excluded. Just as God has pronounced his verdict of condemnation (guilty) on all people because of Adam's fall, so God has pronounced his verdict of justification (not guilty) on all people because of Christ's one act of righteousness. In Christ God "was reconciling the world to himself" (2 Corinthians 5:19). Jesus is "the Lamb of God, who takes away the sin of the world" (John 1:29). God's mercy and grace are all-embracing. Forgiveness of sins is an accomplished fact for every sinner.

This doctrine that God declared all people righteous because of Jesus' perfect life and innocent sufferings and death is called universal and objective justification. We call justification universal because God has forgiven the sins of *all people*. At the same time, justification is objective because it is *an accomplished fact*. God declared the world forgiven when Jesus died for the sins of the world and rose again. God's declaration of forgiveness is true and valid even apart from any human response to it.

God's universal and objective justification is one of the most comforting doctrines of the Bible, because it leaves no doubt in our minds whether we are forgiven. No one has to ask, "Did Jesus die for me?" No one has to worry whether he has somehow fallen through the cracks of God's mercy or whether God forgot him when salvation was obtained for everyone else. The Bible plainly and repeatedly states Jesus earned forgiveness for all. John says, "He is the atoning sacrifice for our sins, and not only for ours but also for the sins of the whole world" (1 John 2:2). Paul says he "gave himself as a ransom for all men" (1 Timothy 2:6).

The importance of faith

At the same time, the Bible also repeatedly speaks of the importance of faith in Jesus. The jailer of Philippi was told, "Believe in the Lord Jesus, and you will be saved" (Acts 16:31). Paul told the Galatians, "The righteous will live by faith" (Galatians 3:11). Jesus said, "Whoever believes and is baptized will be saved, but whoever does not believe will be condemned" (Mark 16:16). From this it can be seen that faith is necessary for salvation.

But what is saving faith? The Bible indicates that saving faith is more than belief in the existence of God (James 2:19). Saving faith is trust in the promises of God and his grace and mercy in Jesus (John 3:16; Romans 4:3). The Lutheran Confessions state simply and correctly that a person has saving faith when he "believes that his sins are forgiven because of Christ."[37]

Individual justification

In discussing faith, we must be careful not to give man the credit for his salvation simply because he believes. Our

Lutheran Confessions put it this way: "Faith does not justify because it is so good a work and so God-pleasing a virtue, but because it lays hold on and accepts the merit of Christ in the promise of the holy Gospel."[38] In other words, God saves us not because we are good, but because he is good and gracious. We are justified not by our own merits or even because of our faith, but only by the merits of Christ.

It is a common misunderstanding among church people today to think, "We are saved *because* we believe." But this is not true. We are not saved by anything we do but only by what God has done for us (Ephesians 2:8,9). Our faith is not the cause of our salvation; it is not a condition we must fulfill in order to be saved.

Faith is not our work but God's! It is not that because God did something important in redeeming mankind, man also must do something great—he must believe. The fact is, God does everything. He redeems us, *and* he gives us the faith we need to claim that redemption for ourselves. Faith is a hand into which God presses the free gift of righteousness from Christ, and it is *a hand that God gives us*! The Bible doctrine that the individual sinner is declared righteous before God when God gives him faith is called individual, or subjective, justification.

Faith is God's miracle

Paul compares conversion to the miracle of creation: "God, who said, 'Let light shine out of darkness,' made his light shine in our hearts to give us the light of the knowledge of the glory of God in the face of Christ" (2 Corinthians 4:6). Just as God made something out of nothing when he created light on the first day of creation, so God made something out of nothing when he put the light of faith into our hearts.

It wasn't that God took some dying embers in our hearts and fanned them into a flame. No, he brought light out of darkness. God alone, without any effort, inclination, predisposition, or cooperation on our part, called us by the gospel of Christ and led us to embrace Jesus in faith as our Lord and Savior. Our coming to faith and our remaining in faith are miracles, just like the miracle God performed when he created light out of darkness. In both cases he made something out of nothing. This biblical teaching of salvation apart from all human efforts and achievements stands in stark contrast to all other religions.

Buddhism: a religion of works

Buddhism is a religion embraced by more than three hundred million people. Buddhists believe that all of human life, that is, all of man's conscious existence, consists of suffering. That suffering is caused by man's desire for life and pleasure. People continue to be reincarnated in a series of lives, and thus continue to suffer, as long as they have a desire for existence. Buddhists' goal is to reach a state of perfection wherein they finally suppress all their passions and desires for life and happiness.

The process by which people can suppress such desires and escape their merry-go-round of misery is called the Eightfold Path: right speech, right conduct, right means of subsistence, right effort, right mindfulness, right meditation, right views, and right intentions. The "right" paths are those that avoid the two extremes of sensuousness and asceticism. Whoever lives this kind of life, adopting the middle path between the two extremes, escapes rebirth and suffering and enters a condition of extinction called

Nirvana, which is the Buddhist state of salvation. Clearly, with its emphasis on working one's way to Nirvana, Buddhism is a religion of works.

Other religions of works

Islam is one of the largest and fastest-growing religions today. Its one billion followers are called Muslims. Though there are many sects in Islam, all Muslims agree that the way to escape punishment and enter paradise on judgment day is by submission to a god they call Allah. Islam is not a religion of faith in a gracious and merciful Savior but, rather, a religion of rules and regulations, duties, pilgrimages, fasting, and almsgiving. Muslims do not have their paradise given to them; they earn it. Like Buddhism, Islam is a religion of works.

In a similar manner, we could investigate all other religions, and we would quickly see that in some way all of them, except Christianity, are religions of works. The Hindus reach their higher level of existence by performing rituals, attaining knowledge, contemplating, or subjecting themselves to severe asceticism. Shinto, a popular religion in Japan, emphasizes rituals and moral standards.

The religion of faith

While all other religions might be described as religions of works, Christianity might be called the religion of faith. All other religions say "do" as the way of salvation. Christianity says, "God has done it." All other religions teach, "Love God and your neighbor, and *then* God will love you." Christianity tells us that God loved us first. All other religions urge us to work hard to get right with God. Christianity teaches that God has already reconciled the world to himself in Christ. All other religions say that salvation must be purchased or earned by human works or merit. Christianity pronounces human works and merit to be entirely inadequate and instead encourages people to trust only in the forgiveness of God earned by the life and merits of Jesus Christ.

According to Christianity, faith in Christ is the only path to glory. In the words of the apostle Paul, "We maintain that a man is justified by faith apart from observing the law" (Romans 3:28).

Man's considerable glory

In this first of three chapters dedicated to the theme "Glory Restored," it is no accident that we have spoken exclusively about what God has done. Even if we had wanted to relate all that man has done to restore himself, we would have nothing to say. We have repeatedly seen that in man's restoration God is the sole rescuer and the only active player, while man by nature is not merely passive but actively hostile toward his benefactor.

This is not to say that man in his restoration is without glory. Consider the infinite value God assigned to mankind when he sent his Son to redeem us, as Luther says in the Small Catechism, "not with gold or silver but with his holy, precious blood and with his innocent suffering and death." Consider the exalted names given to those who are restored through faith in Christ. John calls us "children of God" (1 John 3:1). Paul says, "If we are children, then we are heirs—heirs of God and co-heirs with Christ" (Romans 8:17). Peter says we are "a chosen people, a royal priesthood, a holy nation, a people belonging to God" (1 Peter 2:9). Certainly we who are children of God and have been restored to God's family through faith in Jesus are not without glory!

A *reflected glory*

The glory we have, however, is a reflected glory! It is not an intrinsic glory, one that is ours by nature. It is a glory granted us by grace, because of God's undeserved love for us. It is a glory that demonstrates God's worth and his goodness much more than our own.

We might compare the glory we have with the glory of the moon. As bright and beautiful as the moon is on a clear night, it has no light of its own. The moon shines only by reflecting the light of the sun. In fact, the moon is a very poor reflector, reflecting only about ten percent of the light it receives. It gives only about 1/465,000 as much light as the sun.

In the same way, we Christians have no light of our own. In all that we are and in all that we have and do, we merely reflect the glory of God. And we are not always very good reflectors at that! But if people happen to see something good or honorable in us, they are looking at the reflected glory of God. They are seeing what God has accomplished in us.

10

The Christian's Glorious Struggle

During the course of history, a number of battles have been fought that have had far-reaching effects on subsequent events. History teachers enjoy pointing out how different the world might be today if those battles had gone another way. The political structure of our world and even civilization itself might be much different. Most of us remember from our study of history the importance of the battle of Gettysburg during the Civil War or the battles of Stalingrad, Normandy, and Midway in the Second World War.

Going back earlier in history, what if the Mongols had swept over all of Europe in the 13th century? Or what if the Muslim Turks had surged over all of Europe in the late

14th century or in the 16th century? Would Europe have retained its Christianity? Would there even be a European civilization as we know it today? What a difference the outcome of strategic battles can make!

Our Savior's battles

Now think of the battles our Savior won for us. Think of how different our future would be if those battles had gone another way. For 33 years our Lord Jesus faced the onslaughts of Satan's temptations but never yielded. He did not shrink back from the ultimate sacrifice. He did not plead youth or innocence or even divine privilege but went to the cross because the Father asked him to do so. Jesus was a good soldier. He fought the battles he was sent to fight. We shudder to think of our predicament if he hadn't.

The spoils of victory

To the victors of war go the spoils. When Jesus won the victory over sin and death, the spoils of his victory were not wealth or territory but precious souls—us. He liberated us that we might serve him. Paul tells us, "He died for all, that those who live should no longer live for themselves but for him who died for them and was raised again" (2 Corinthians 5:15). Now that we are set free from sin, we have become "slaves to God" (Romans 6:22).

The thought of being spoils of victory and slaves to God may not seem very attractive, until we realize that no one has benefited more from Jesus' victory than we have. We not only *are* the spoils; we *share in* the spoils. Because of Jesus God no longer regards us as his enemies; we are his friends. Because of Jesus we are no longer foreigners; we are citizens of God's kingdom. We are no longer children of Satan, but God's beloved sons and daughters, heirs of all his blessings.

Our changed relationships

Few things more dramatically illustrate the change in our relationship with God than the fact that we are able to pray. Since Holy Scripture describes as true prayers only those that are offered to God through Jesus or in the name of Jesus, only the prayers of Christians are answered by God (John 14:6; 16:23). The Bible says, "The eyes of the Lord are on the righteous and his ears are attentive to their prayer, but the face of the Lord is against those who do evil" (1 Peter 3:12).

Like children loved by their parents, Christians know they can confidently bring any matters to the attention of their heavenly Father and expect that God will hear and answer their prayers. Therefore Christians pray continuously (1 Thessalonians 5:17). The Spirit also prays for Christians even when they don't know what to pray (Romans 8:26,27).

When we become Christians, a change takes place in our relationships with other people also. For the first time, we know what love really is. We have seen perfect love in action at the cross. We know that love is not that nice, warm feeling we have when other people make us happy; love is our desire to make others happy. Love is our willingness to sacrifice ourselves for others just as Jesus sacrificed himself for us. Love is our desire to give of ourselves rather than our desire to receive.

Glory restored

As God's dear children through faith in Jesus, we have come full circle: from glory to ashes and back. We saw earlier how man was created in glory and in the very image of God, privileged to live in God's loving presence. We saw how that glorious future went up in flames when Adam and Eve fell into sin and man's hopes were reduced to ashes. But now through Jesus' victory and the Holy Spirit's gift of faith, man's glory is restored.

Can it really be? Can we poor mortals really possess glory of any kind? We certainly can! The Bible tells us that through faith we once again possess the holiness Adam lost when he fell into sin. Through faith God credits to our account the perfect righteousness of Christ (Romans 4:3,23,24). Paul says, "God made him who had no sin to be sin for us, so that in him we might become the righteousness of God" (2 Corinthians 5:21). Notice that we don't merely *have* righteousness, which might easily slip through our fingers and be lost, but we actually *become* that righteousness. And it's not some incomplete or tainted righteousness that we become, but the *righteousness of God*.

A new attitude

Faith in Christ not only gives us righteousness before God; it also gives us an entirely different attitude toward everything. Our whole way of thinking is changed. The gospel, which we once regarded as the greatest foolishness, we now esteem as the highest wisdom. The Bible, which we once could either take or leave, we now regard as dearer than life. The troubles and difficulties of life, which once filled us with frustration and disappointment, now produce perseverance, character, and hope (Romans 5:3,4). We rejoice in tribulation, knowing that "in all things God works for the good of those who love him" (8:28).

The thought of death and judgment, which once paralyzed our hearts with fear, no longer frightens us. In fact, as judgment day approaches, we look up and rejoice because our "redemption is drawing near" (Luke 21:28). Even the thought of being slaves to God is no longer humiliating or disgraceful to us. We want nothing more than the opportunity to "serve him [God] without fear in holiness and righteousness before him all our days" (1:74,75). Paul sums up the tremendous difference the restoration of God's image makes in us when he describes the Christian as a new creation: "If anyone is in Christ, he is a new creation; the old has gone, the new has come" (2 Corinthians 5:17).

This new attitude in us, which helps us see everything in a completely different light, the Bible calls our new self (Ephesians 4:24). It is also called the new man, the inner being, and the spirit (Ezekiel 11:19; Romans 7:22).

The battles within

The new man within us is not without opposition. In addition to the new man, we still have the old man, the sinful nature all people inherit from Adam. In respect to the new man, the believer is perfectly holy and needs no improvement (Romans 7:22). In respect to the old man, the Christian is no better than the most degenerate unbeliever (Romans 7:18).

The old man clings to us as long as we live in this world. It is a powerful force, struggling against faith and conscience, against truth and honesty and everything good. It has only one goal, to bring us back under the slavery of sin so that we lose faith and ultimately heaven itself. Paul says: "The sinful nature desires what is contrary to the Spirit, and the Spirit what is contrary to the sinful nature. They are in conflict with each other, so that you do not do what you want" (Galatians 5:17).

As the old man and the new man compete for mastery, the Christian's inner life becomes a ceaseless struggle, a never-ending series of battles. Sometimes the new man seems to be winning. At other times it seems as if the old man is in control and the new man has no strength at all. Even the apostle Paul lamented how often he failed to live as a Christian should. So strong was the old man in him that he said, "What I do is not the good I want to do; no, the evil I do not want to do—this I keep on doing" (Romans 7:19). He went on to utter a cry of distress: "What a wretched man I am! Who will rescue me from this body of death?" (Romans 7:24). Who will deliver me from this sinful flesh of mine, which is determined to drag me down into sin and eternal death?

The meaning of the struggle

Every Christian has the experience of the apostle Paul: the good he wants to do, he doesn't do, and the evil he doesn't want to do, he does. At the beginning of a day, we may make a solemn promise to God that we will do everything we can to help other people, we will say nothing to hurt anyone, we will not spread or listen to any gossip, and we will not curse or swear. But what happens? The good we want to do, we don't do, and the evil we don't want to do, we do.

Does the battle within mean we aren't Christians? Nothing could be farther from the truth. The battle within is evidence that we *are* Christians. If there were no battle, we could assume the new man is dead and faith is gone, since the old man no longer has any opposition. But since a battle is going on, we know the new man is alive!

It is significant that the Bible never describes believers as people who are perfect or who never sin or even as people for whom the struggle with sin is easy. Believers sometimes stumble, stagger, and go in the wrong direction. But as the Holy Spirit daily renews the new man, Christians are not satisfied with their behavior. They repent of their sins. They change direction. They renew the battle against sin.

Saint and sinner at the same time

Luther repeatedly pointed out that the Christian is "saint and sinner at the same time."[39] Believers are saints, or holy persons, because their sins are freely forgiven through the merits of Christ. But believers are also weak and often overwhelmed by their sinful flesh.

In his lectures on Genesis, Luther pointed out that even the greatest saints often fell into sin. Noah became drunk. Lot and his daughters committed incest. Rachel worshiped idols. When Judah wrongfully refused his widowed daughter-in-law, Tamar, her right to marry his son Shelah, she tricked Judah to have sexual intercourse with her that she might have a child by him. Luther said:

> Such sins of the saints are recounted at such length and so fully for our comfort, to the end that we may know that the patriarchs and saintly matrons were like us. Sometimes they accomplished great and sublime things that we can by no means attain or imitate. Things of this kind are recorded in the Epistle to the Hebrews [11:4-40]. Sometimes, however, they perpetrated foolish, ridiculous, yes, the very worst of outrageous sins, in order that God alone might be glorified in our works, both good and evil—in the good works which he himself has done in us and in the evil works which he has forgiven in his mercy.[40]

Our weapon

God has given us only one weapon against Satan, the old man, and sin, but it is a devastating weapon: his Word. Through God's Word Jesus overcame the temptations of the devil (Matthew 4:1-11). Through his Word the saints of old were kept in faith. When they lost a battle with sin, God's promise of love and forgiveness raised them up to fight again.

Paul told the Corinthians: "The weapons we fight with are not the weapons of the world. On the contrary, they have divine power to demolish strongholds" (2 Corinthians 10:4). God's Word is a defensive weapon, shielding us against sin and error (Psalm 119:9; Titus 1:9), and an offensive weapon, "the sword of the Spirit" (Ephesians 6:17), enabling us to storm the very stronghold of the enemy.

The folly of disarmament

Peace movements sometimes advocate unilateral disarmament. Such a policy ignores the reality of man's cruelty to man and leaves a nation defenseless against its enemies. Many Christians disarm themselves spiritually by finding little or no time for hearing and learning the Word of God. Without God's Word they have no answer to temptation and despair. They have no protection against the attacks of their spiritual enemies.

Luther once said that life in this world should be like that of a man staying for the night in an inn or hotel.[41] The man discovers that the place where he is staying is a den of robbers, a place where people steal from and even kill the travelers who come. When the man finds that out, he doesn't sleep very soundly, knowing that at any moment someone might break in to steal his belongings and take his life. In the same way, Luther said, you and I live in a hostile environment. This is not only God's world but also the home of the devil, where he walks about seeking those whom he may devour (1 Peter 5:8). We are in a state of war. We are in danger. We cannot afford to sleep soundly. We cannot lay down our weapons.

Severing our supply lines

When at war, as we are, it is important to know the enemy's skills and tactics. One of the strategies modern armies use is to disrupt their opponent's supply lines. If the enemy bombs your factories back home or severs your supply lines to keep arms and ammunition from arriving at the front, you will lose the war. Similarly, the old man likes nothing better than to invent excuses to keep us away from church services and the Word of God. He works hard to disrupt our spiritual supply lines and to keep us from feeding our faith.

A soldier cannot fight if he is not fed. The believer is commonly pictured in the Bible as a plant or tree that needs to be watered and nourished so it might grow (Psalm 1). The nourishment God provides for faith is the gospel in Word and sacrament (Romans 10:17). Through diligent use of the gospel, believers grow strong in their faith and in spiritual knowledge (Colossians 2:6,7). Good works are the result of the good nourishment they receive (John 15:5). And as the new man grows in strength, the old man weakens (Romans 6).

Propaganda

The old man is good at psychological warfare and propaganda. Just as a modern army drops propaganda leaflets behind enemy lines to weaken its opponent's morale and destroy his will to fight, so the old man uses propaganda in the form of lies, temptations, and false doctrines.

The old man wages a clever war of words. Before he leads us into sin, the old man minimizes its importance. He tries to persuade us that sin is very small: "Everyone is doing it. There is no danger. God doesn't care. Just do it once and find out what it's like; you can always repent later." After we have sinned, Satan begins to picture sin as very big: "Do you realize what you've done? God will never forgive you for that!" He hopes to lead us into despair.

The old man also wages guerrilla warfare, a war of attrition in which he slowly wears us down. He doesn't always try to win big battles. He's content to win little battles, chipping away at us bit by bit. He knows that if we lose enough of the little battles, we'll soon lose the big battles as well. If "Honesty Hill" isn't important enough to fight for, perhaps "Morality Mountain" won't be worth fighting for either. If the little sins aren't worth resisting, finally no territory will be worth fighting for. Again, the goal is to erode our resistance, to get us used to sin, so that losing even the big battles won't matter after a while.

Know the enemy's voice

Most of us have a multitude of opinions on a wide variety of topics. We don't always agree with one another regarding these opinions, whether the subject be politics or matters of ethics. In addition, the ideas and opinions we hold may change over a period of time.

It isn't just new information that changes our minds about things. Sometimes our change of thinking may be due to the up-again, down-again struggle between the old man and new man. When the old man is in control, we think differently than when the new man is in control.

Having this dual influence of the old man and new man has been compared to having both hot and cold water come out of a single water faucet.[42] One time the water that comes out is hot. Another time it is cold. What we turn on is what we get! It would be a mistake not to monitor and control the temperature of the water that comes out of a faucet. Everything from hands to goldfish has been burned by water that was too hot.

Similarly, it would be a mistake to ignore the source of the thoughts that pour out of our minds. We need to ask: "Who is talking? The old man or the new? God's enemy or God's friend?" It would be a mistake for us to issue a blanket acceptance for all our ideas and opinions simply because they come from us, without subjecting them to spiritual review. Sometimes that voice in our minds is not us as Christians, it is the sinful nature!

Identifying friend and foe

The voices of the old man and the new man can be identified on the basis of their results. The old man, for example, hates to hear about money from the pulpit. The old man cries "Foul!" whenever the sermon application strikes a little too close to home. The new man, on the other hand, not only doesn't object to the subject of money but *wants* to hear what God's Word says about it. The new man knows that everything he has comes from God and still belongs to God. The new man looks for encouragement and suggestions on how to improve his service to God even if that suggestion touches his wallet.

The old man encourages us to be judgmental concerning our neighbor. The new man "keeps no record of wrongs"

(1 Corinthians 13:5). The old man urges us to be dissatis-fied with our lot in life. The new man is content with what he has, "because God has said, 'Never will I leave you; never will I forsake you'" (Hebrews 13:5). The old man counsels laziness and neglect. The new man urges us to work as long as it is day, because "night is coming, when no one can work" (John 9:4). The old man tries to drive a wedge of hostility between us and our pastor, between us and our church. The new man urges us to honor "those whose work is preaching and teaching" (1 Timothy 5:17) and to love our brothers (1 John 3:14-16).

Between two great victories

When the apostle Paul felt great distress, when he saw himself losing far too many battles, he said: "What a wretched man I am! Who will rescue me from this body of death?" (Romans 7:24). But then he quickly added, "Thanks be to God—through Jesus Christ our Lord!" (verse 25). God has fought for us through Jesus. When we were helpless, Jesus was our champion and Savior. At Calvary Jesus silenced any charge of sin that any-one might have leveled against us (8:33). At his Easter tomb, he conquered death so that it lost its sting (1 Cor-inthians 15:55). His victory was complete, thorough, and overwhelming.

But if the victory Jesus won is complete, why are we still fighting? Why are the battles still raging? Part of the answer is, we are not dealing with an ordinary enemy. Though the enemy has been defeated, he fights as if he doesn't know he has lost. In anger and desperation, he continues to press us hard. Though doomed to failure by the power of God himself, he continues to pry at the doors of our hearts.

Our situation is like that of the U.S. Marines on Guadalcanal in World War II. After some 80 days of bitter fighting, the Marines won a great victory on that island. The enemy's back was broken. But that didn't end the fighting. Marine reinforcements had to be sent in for a mop-up campaign. Many more Marines were killed and wounded before the final victory, when the last enemy surrendered. So we too live between two great victories: Good Friday/Easter and judgment day. Many battles must still be fought. Many temptations must be overcome. Many of us will be hurting before it is all over. But God, who has already conquered our spiritual enemies, will see us through to victory.

A life of glorious hope

In our portrayal of the Christian's life in this chapter, we have been frank and honest. Our lives are not all sunshine and laughter. They are also full of conflict, pain, and trouble. Every one of us has to bear a cross in his lifetime. Temptations, failures, sickness, disability, loss of property, loss of loved ones and various other disappointments may trouble us at one time or another. Yet for the Christian even such an imperfect and often dissatisfying life is buoyed by a glorious hope. We hope and trust in God for his guidance and protection while we live in this world. We hope and trust in his promise that he will temper our afflictions and temptations so they will never overwhelm our faith (1 Corinthians 10:13).

What's more, our hope is not limited to this life! We have a hope that extends beyond the grave. God "has given us new birth into a living hope through the resurrection of Jesus Christ from the dead, and into an inheritance that can never perish, spoil, or fade" (1 Peter 1:3,4).

Heaven awaits us. Therefore we say with Paul: "We do not lose heart. Though outwardly we are wasting away, yet inwardly we are being renewed day by day. For our light and momentary troubles are achieving for us an eternal glory that far outweighs them all" (2 Corinthians 4:16,17).

In the next chapter we will see more clearly how great that glory will be.

11

The Glory That Awaits Us in Heaven

It happens more often than we would like to admit. We find ourselves on the wrong side of a locked door. We reach into our pockets and suddenly realize we don't have the keys for the house or car. We may have all kinds of keys, but not the right one. It's only a simple lock, but locks are made to keep people out. We may have to break a window or call a family member to bring a key. Whatever the solution, it's a terrible, sinking feeling to be on the wrong side of a locked door.

Locking ourselves out of a house or car can be frustrating, but what have we really lost? A little time? A little pride? A broken window? In most cases we probably can afford the loss. But how tragic it would be if one day we found ourselves locked out of heaven! No one can afford to be on the wrong side of heaven's locked door.

Perhaps it seems strange to think of heaven as having a door with a lock on it. But when Jesus told his disciples he would give them "the keys of the kingdom of heaven" (Matthew 16:19), he encouraged them to think of heaven as a place with a lock and a key. The lock on heaven's door is sin. The key is the precious gospel of Christ. When we believe that Jesus' innocent death on the cross won God's full forgiveness for us, the door of heaven swings open for us.

Death is not the end

Temporal death is not the end of man's existence. Even most of those who know nothing about the Bible sense that man's conscious existence and personal identity continue beyond the grave. Not only Christianity but almost every man-made religion as well speaks of an existence after death. The Hindus speak of reincarnation, the Muslims of sensual paradise, and the Mormons of becoming gods.

While the heathen can only guess at the existence of life after death, the Christian knows with certainty that such a life exists. Both the Old and New Testaments clearly teach that death is not the end. Job knew that on judgment day he would be alive to see God (Job 19:26). When the Sadducees ridiculed the idea of a resurrection, Jesus reminded them that in the Old Testament, God had called himself "the God of Abraham, and the God of Isaac, and the God of Jacob" (Luke 20:37,38; Exodus 3:6). Abraham, Isaac, and Jacob had died centuries before. Yet God spoke of his relationship with them as continuing. This only could mean they were still alive.

Jesus often spoke of the soul living on after death. He told his disciples not to be afraid of humans, who cannot kill the soul (Matthew 10:28). His story of the rich man and Lazarus (Luke 16:19-31) and his description of the final judgment (Matthew 25:31-46) were based on the fact that temporal death is not the end of man's personal existence.

Peter spoke of the wicked living on after death and described them as "spirits in prison" (1 Peter 3:19). John pictured the righteous standing before the throne singing praises to God (Revelation 7:9,10). It would be impossible for anyone who denies the existence of life after death to claim acceptance of the Bible's teachings.

What happens to the soul?

The Bible tells us that when a person dies, "the spirit returns to God who gave it" (Ecclesiastes 12:7). The apostle Paul said, "I desire to depart and be with Christ" (Philippians 1:23). Paul was confident that when he died he would be "at home with the Lord" (2 Corinthians 5:8). From this it is evident that when believers die, their souls are with God in heaven.

There is no basis for the idea that the souls of the dead remain on earth to communicate with the living. The souls of the dead apparently are ignorant of us (Isaiah 63:16). They do not leave heaven even temporarily to warn the wicked (Luke 16:27-29). The souls of the dead are not absorbed into the essence of God in heaven, as many have suggested, but they continue to exist as separate, personal entities (Luke 20:37,38).

Death as a sleep

The Bible repeatedly speaks of death as a sleep, to call attention to the fact that death is not permanent (Daniel

12:2; John 11:11). Just as we awaken from sleep, so we will awaken from death.

However, only the body sleeps in death, not the soul. It would be a mistake to imagine a "soul sleep," in which our souls are deprived of an immediate enjoyment of God and the blessings of heaven. Jesus told the thief crucified with him, "*Today* you will be with me in paradise" (Luke 23:43). John wrote, "Blessed are the dead who die in the Lord *from now on*" (Revelation 14:13). In other words, those who die trusting in Jesus are happy immediately. On the other hand, those who die without faith begin to suffer the torments of hell immediately (Luke 16:22-24).

The resurrection of the body

The ancient Greek philosophers Pythagoras and Plato taught that the soul is the only real or lasting part of our being.[43] They taught that while the soul lives in this world, it is imprisoned in the body as a kind of punishment. Eventually the soul gains its freedom at death. Its goal is to reach such a great degree of purity that it never again is forced to live in a body.

Such thinking does injustice to the body. The body too is a creation of God. Though the body returns at death to the ground it came from (Ecclesiastes 12:7), it too is intended by God to enjoy a blessed eternity with him. God promises that on judgment day he will raise our bodies and reunite them with our souls (Acts 24:15; 2 Corinthians 1:9).

The resurrection of Jesus proves that there will be a resurrection of our bodies on judgment day. Christ was "the first fruits" harvested from the grave, and the rest of us will follow (1 Corinthians 15:20). While on earth, Jesus proved his power over death by raising a widow's son (Luke 7:15), the daughter of Jairus (Matthew 9:25), and his friend Lazarus (John 11:43,44). When he comes on the Last Day, he will demonstrate his power over death by raising *all* the dead. On the Last Day, "all who are in their graves will hear his voice and come out—those who have done good will rise to live, and those who have done evil will rise to be condemned" (John 5:28,29).

We will recognize one another

John speaks of the "great and small, standing before the throne" in heaven (Revelation 20:12). It is unclear whether "great and small" refers to children and adults or leaders and common people. If John is referring to physical stature, the passage is evidence that our resurrected bodies will be the same bodies we have now. If we were tall in this life, we will be tall in heaven. If we were short here, we will be short there.

Whatever "great and small" means, there are other indications that the bodies we have after the resurrection will be the same bodies we had before we died. Jesus did not have the body of a stranger at his resurrection. His disciples recognized him because of the nail marks and the wounds in his side. Job knew that even though he would die and his body would decay, in the resurrection he would have the same body he had in this life: "After my skin has been destroyed, yet in my flesh I will see God; I myself will see him with my own eyes—I, and not another" (Job 19:26,27). All this assures us that our identities will be preserved in heaven and we will have the same bodies there that we had here.

Our bodies glorified

Even though our resurrected bodies will be the same bodies we had in this life, they will have new qualities and characteristics. Paul tells us Christ "will transform our lowly bodies so that they will be like his glorious body" (Philippians 3:21). Believers who are living at the second coming of Christ will have their bodies changed in a moment (1 Corinthians 15:51,52).

Our present bodies are subject to weakness, sickness, pain, and aging. They have defects and deformities. Many of us wear glasses, hearing aids, artificial limbs, or pacemakers. Many people depend on medicine to keep their fragile bodies alive. When someone dies, we bury the body quickly, before the smell of decay offends our senses and the contamination of rotting flesh ruins our health! As Paul says, our present flesh and blood are perishable and not fit to dwell in heaven (1 Corinthians 15:50). But although "the body that is sown is perishable, it is raised imperishable; it is sown in dishonor, it is raised in glory; it is sown in weakness, it is raised in power; it is sown a natural body, it is raised a spiritual body" (verses 42-44). Our new "spiritual bodies," as Paul calls them, will have all their previous deficiencies removed. Every weakness and defect will be erased.

It is hard to imagine bodies that are perfect, but that's what we will have in heaven, bodies no longer subject to disease and crippling, bodies without extra pounds, bodies that never feel hunger, thirst, or any kind of discomfort (Revelation 7:16), bodies that never grow tired, bodies that are forever young. All the effects of sin will be gone. All this is contained in God's promise that "there will be no more death or mourning or crying or pain, for the old order of things has passed away" (21:4).

As a plant differs from its seed

Paul says the bodies we have in the resurrection will be different from the bodies we have now just as a plant differs from the seed from which it grows: "Someone may ask, 'How are the dead raised? With what kind of body will they come?' How foolish! What you sow does not come to life unless it dies. When you sow, you do not plant the body that will be, but just a seed, perhaps of wheat or of something else. But God gives it a body as he has determined, and to each kind of seed he gives its own body" (1 Corinthians 15:35-38).

How, then, will we recognize one another if our bodies are so thoroughly changed? Siegbert Becker commented on this: "Someone who has never seen corn and other plants grow might find it very difficult to believe that an eight-foot cornstalk with a large ear grew from a tiny yellow bit of protoplasm. But those who have had experience in such matters will recognize the tiny green plant as corn when they see it, even if its color and its form is not at all like the kernel of corn that was planted."[44]

What exactly will our bodies look like in heaven? It is obvious that the answer to this and many other questions will have to wait until we reach heaven. The fact that our resurrected bodies will be the same bodies we had in this life is clear. The exact qualities and appearance of those bodies is unclear. The fact that we will recognize one another in heaven is clear. How we will recognize one another is unclear. John says: "What we will be has not yet been made known. But we know that when he appears, we shall be like him, for we shall see him as he is" (1 John 3:2).

No sin in heaven

The changes in our resurrected bodies are directly connected with the absence of sin. We know that death must exist wherever sin is, because death is the wages of sin (Romans 6:23). Because death is absent from heaven, we know that sin will be absent. In heaven believers will be confirmed in their bliss. A fall into sin will be impossible once we have reached the glory of heaven.

How can this be? How can people who are so sinful here on earth become perfectly righteous in heaven? Remember that our spiritual enemies will no longer be present to tempt and deceive us. Satan will be thrown into the lake of burning sulfur (Revelation 20:10). The old man will be completely removed and discarded (Ephesians 5:27). The new man will no longer have the old man beclouding it and refusing to let it rule. Our knowledge of God finally will be perfect. All our questions and doubts about God and his will will be answered in heaven. Paul says: "Now we see but a poor reflection as in a mirror; then we shall see face to face. Now I know in part; then I shall know fully, even as I am fully known" (1 Corinthians 13:12).

Beatific vision

No doubt the most captivating and thrilling experience we will have in heaven will be seeing God face to face. This blessing of seeing God in all his goodness and glory theologians call the beatific vision. The psalmist speaks of this joyful and blissful sight when he says to God, "In righteousness I will see your face; when I awake, *I will be satisfied with seeing your likeness*" (Psalm 17:15). The psalmist says he will be entirely satisfied when he sees God's face. He will be supremely happy and contented.

So it will be for us. The sight of God in all his glory will be so fulfilling for us that we too will be entirely sat- isfied. We will have no desire to seek some higher good than God. We will have no yearning to turn our attentions to anything better, because there will be nothing better. This also explains in part the absence of sin in heaven. We will be so satisfied with the sight of God in heaven that we will have no desire to do anything but gaze upon God and do his will. It's not that God will pre-vent us from sinning by his almighty power but that we will have no desire to sin.

Heaven's joys

We have seen what heaven is not: no sin, no trouble, no imperfection, no crying, no pain, no death. But God also tells us what heaven is like in positive terms. He com-pares heaven to certain happy experiences people have in this life. For example, heaven is compared to a great res-cue (1 Thessalonians 1:10; Revelation 7:14-17). If we have ever been saved or rescued from some great danger, we have had a foretaste of heaven.

Heaven is also called a rest (Hebrews 4:9,10). If we have ever had an extremely long and exhausting day of work and then suddenly were finished and could sit down and rest, we have had a foretaste of heaven.

Heaven is also compared to receiving an inheritance (Revelation 21:7). If we have ever received an undeserved and unexpected inheritance, we have had a foretaste of heaven. In this way God compares heaven to many enjoy-able experiences: living in a house with many rooms (John 14:2), attending a wedding banquet (Matthew 25:10), reigning like a king (Revelation 22:5), and eating a great feast (Luke 22:30).

Wonderment and anticipation

In spite of everything we know about heaven, it is still difficult for us to understand. It's not that God can't tell us what heaven is like but that our comprehension is limited. As Wilbert Gawrisch put it, "We are like an old woman with cataracts on her eyes who can barely make out the form of her grandchildren, even though they are standing in the bright noonday sun."[45]

Having spent many years in this imperfect world, it's hard for us to imagine a world with no death, sorrow, or pain. It's hard to imagine a world without temptation and sin. It's hard to imagine a world without mental illness, depression, failure, hunger, and thirst. It's hard to imagine a world where doctors, nurses, and hospitals are no longer needed. It's hard to imagine a world without marriage (Matthew 22:30) and separate families, a world without government for the punishment of the wicked, a world where mission work is no longer necessary.

No matter how much we know about heaven, many questions of wonderment and anticipation go unanswered. We find ourselves asking:

- What will it be like to fall asleep one day and then to wake up and find ourselves in heaven?

- What will it be like to see Jesus face to face?

- What will it be like to see and talk with angels?

- What will it be like to exchange loneliness and suffering for everlasting happiness and contentment in the presence of God?

- What will it be like to exchange fleeting time for endless eternity?

- What will it be like to cast aside mortality and exchange it for immortality?

- What will it be like to live in a place where people are forever young, where people never grow weary?

- What will it be like to be reunited with Christian loved ones after many long years without them?

- What will it be like to mingle with the saints of old, with Moses and Abraham, Elijah and John the Baptist?

Our joy complete

Yes, what will it be like in heaven? Obviously, heaven will be a beautiful place, far more satisfying than anything we have ever experienced and more wonderful than anything we can imagine. In heaven we will be gloriously happy, living with God in close and continual fellowship (Revelation 21:3). In his presence there will be complete satisfaction, perfect contentment, and absolute safety (John 10:28). In his presence we will be filled with joy (Psalm 16:11). We will be undisturbed and unmolested by any evil.

Who can comprehend the glories of heaven? Here sin is everywhere; there holiness and purity abound. Here everyone sins; there no one sins. Here everyone experiences pain and sorrow; there our joy will be complete.

God's purpose in telling us

Surely we will want to be in heaven someday. In fact, that is why God has told us about heaven. It's not that God wants us to argue endlessly about where heaven is located or about the exact form and appearance of our glorified bodies or about what God will look like when we see him. No, God has told us about heaven so that we will live in such a way that we do not lose the glory that awaits us there (Matthew 25:1-13). Our knowledge of heaven's glory is an incentive for us to believe the gospel and persevere in faith. It cheers us as we travel through this vale of tears.

Another reason why God has told us about heaven is so that we might be active in helping other people get there.

Remember how Jesus wept over Jerusalem (Luke 19:41) and how he had compassion on the crowd that came to hear him, because they were like sheep without a shepherd (Mark 6:34). Remember when Jesus said: "What good is it for a man to gain the whole world, yet forfeit his soul? Or what can a man give in exchange for his soul?" (Mark 8:36,37). Jesus' love for souls prompted him to commission his disciples of all times to "go and make disciples of all nations" (Matthew 28:19). How flattered we are that he has entrusted this great work to us! And how eager we are to do it!

The obituaries

One of the things you can learn from obituaries is the fact that every day the world loses a tremendous amount of talent and some truly important people. If you look through a newspaper like the *Chicago Tribune*, for example, which doesn't print just any obituary, you don't have to look very long before you find the obituaries of people who were presidents of companies or officers of local civic organizations. You can find financiers, inventors, authors, and artists.

However, an obituary alone will never be able to measure a person's real importance. No newspaper in Paul's day would have been able to measure Paul's real importance to the world or the value of the souls he helped save. If there had been an obituary column in Paul's day to report his death, what would it have said? Perhaps something very uncomplimentary, like this: "Paul of Tarsus, Roman citizen, educated under Gamaliel, religious fanatic and follower of Jesus, beheaded for his crimes against the state."

So it is today. Christians may not always make it to the top of their companies or serve in any important offices.

They may never become well known. Yet their importance to the world is far greater than obituaries would have us believe. Every Christian has the greatest responsibility in the world as a witness and missionary for Christ. If Christians do everything they can to help others reach the safety of heaven, if they do their work faithfully as witnesses for Christ, their accomplishments will be far greater than most people realize.

Our real importance

Someday we too will die. Our obituaries will appear in the newspapers. Perhaps people will read them with interest. They'll say: "That's the person I went to school with. . . . That's the person who lived on Mulberry Street." They'll see the offices we held, our accomplishments, and the years we worked at one place or another. But from our obituaries they will never be able to determine our real importance in this world.

That will be recorded in the book of life, where the names of those we helped on the road to heaven by our encouragements, instructions, prayers, good examples, and invitations will appear. In the book of life will be listed not how many people or how much money we left behind, but the names of those we brought with us. That's all that will matter then, and that's what matters most now. Therein lies life's true importance! Therein we busy ourselves with the purpose God had in mind for us from the beginning, that we might serve and glorify him who deserves our praise.

Claim your inheritance!

Once there was a man who inherited a great estate in a faraway country. He was notified of his inheritance, but he never went to take possession of it. He knew very little about his inheritance and never cared to know. Though he was living in poverty and deprivation, he never thought about the estate he had inherited. He was content to pour his energy and thoughts into the slum of trouble and disappointment where he lived. He could have lived in wealth beyond his wildest dreams, but he loved the life he had.

Such are those who never think about their heavenly inheritance, whose lives and energies are expended on the poverty of this earthly existence. Though they could live in the castle of God's grace and wisdom, they are content to dwell in the broken-down shacks of their earthly hopes and dreams.

What a difference our eternal salvation can make in our lives if we remember to draw daily comfort from it! How unnecessary are so many of the tears we shed because we pay more attention to our troubles now than the heaven that is waiting for us! Let us claim our inheritance! Through faith let us begin to enjoy it even now! There *is* a heaven. There *is* glory in our future.

In the heaven that awaits us the story of man comes full circle. Our gracious God created us in glory. When we became ashes, he did not desert us. Through Christ and through no merit of our own, he has brought us back to glory. From glory to ashes and back. A happy ending provided by the God who loves us. Let us join our voices with the apostle Paul and with countless saints and angels and say, "To him be glory for ever and ever. Amen" (2 Timothy 4:18).

Endnotes

[1]Corliss Lamont, *The Philosophy of Humanism* (New York: Continuum, 1990), pp. 292,293.

[2]Abraham Maslow, *Toward a Psychology of Being* (New York: Van Norstrand Reinhold Co., 1968), p. 4.

[3]Raymond F. Surburg, "In the Beginning God Created," in *Darwin, Evolution, and Creation*, edited by Paul A. Zimmerman (St. Louis: Concordia Publishing House, 1959), p. 56.

[4]Charles Darwin, *The Origin of Species by Means of Natural Selection* (New York: Avenel Books, 1979), pp. 458,459.

[5]Philip Appleman, *Darwin—A Norton Critical Edition* (New York: W. W. Norton & Company, Inc., 1970), pp. 269,270.

[6]Appleman, p. 270.

[7]Appleman, p. 276.

[8]Surburg, p. 39.

[9]Large Catechism, Part I:3, *The Book of Concord: The Confessions of the Evangelical Lutheran Church*, translated and edited by Theodore G. Tappert (Philadelphia: Fortress Press, 1959), p. 365.

[10]*Journal of Discourses*, Vol. VI, p. 5.

[11]*Journal of Discourses*, Vol. VI, p. 3.

[12]Walter Martin, *The Kingdom of the Cults* (Minneapolis: Bethany Fellowship, Inc., 1977), p. 178.

[13]Wallace F. Bennett, *Why I Am A Mormon* (New York: Thomas Nelson & Sons, 1958), pp. 184,185.

[14]Martin Luther, *Luther's Works*, edited by Jaroslav Pelikan and Helmut T. Lehmann, American Edition, Vol. 1 (St. Louis: Concordia Publishing House; Philadelphia: Fortress Press, 1955–1986), p. 95.

[15]John C. Jeske, *Genesis* of The People's Bible series (Milwaukee: Northwestern Publishing House, 1991), p. 45.

[16]Hans Schwarz, *Our Cosmic Journey* (Minneapolis: Augsburg Publishing House, 1977), p. 177.

[17]Formula of Concord, Epitome, Article VI:2, Tappert, p. 480.

[18]Formula of Concord, Solid Declaration, Article V:17, Tappert, p. 561.

[19]Pope Pius IX, *Ineffabilis Deus: Apostolic Constitution Defining the Dogma of the Immaculate Conception* (Boston: St. Paul Books & Media, no date), p. 8.

[20]Formula of Concord, Solid Declaration, Article I:7, Tappert, p. 510.

[21]Formula of Concord, Solid Declaration, Article I:10-13, Tappert, pp. 510,511.

[22]Francis Pieper, *Christian Dogmatics* (St. Louis: Concordia Publishing House, 1950), Vol. I, p. 539.

[23]Formula of Concord, Epitome, Article I:4, Tappert, p. 466.

[24]Formula of Concord, Epitome, Article, Article I:8, Tappert, p. 467.

[25]Formula of Concord, Solid Declaration, Article I:5, Tappert, p. 509.

[26]Edward W. A. Koehler, *A Summary of Christian Doctrine* (St. Louis: Concordia Publishing House, 1952), pp. 65,66.

[27]John A. Hardon, *The Question and Answer Catholic Catechism* (Doubleday & Company, Inc: Garden City, New York, 1981), p. 186.

[28]Hardon, p. 187.

[29]Formula of Concord, Solid Declaration, Article II:12, Tappert, p. 522.

[30]Desiderius Erasmus, *On the Freedom of the Will*, translated and edited by E. Gordon Rupp in *Luther and Erasmus: Free Will and Salvation* of The Library of Christian Classics, Vol. 17, (Philadelphia: Westminster, 1969), p. 96.

[31]*Luther's Works*, Vol. 33, pp. 65,66.

[32]*Luther's Works*, Vol. 33, pp. 226-228.

[33]*Luther's Works*, Vol. 33, p. 294.

[34]Piet Schoonenberg, *Man And Sin* (Notre Dame: Notre Dame Press, 1965), pp. 74,75.

[35]Edward W. A. Koehler, *A Summary of Christian Doctrine*, p. 124.

[36]Formula of Concord, Solid Declaration, Article I:11, Tappert, p. 510.

[37]Apology of the Augsburg Confession, Article IV:45, Tappert, p. 113.

[38]Formula of Concord, Solid Declaration, Article III:13, Tappert, p. 541.

[39]*Luther's Works*, Vol. 26, p. 232; Vol. 27, p. 231.

[40]*Luther's Works*, Vol. 7, p. 28.

[41]*Luther's Works*, Vol. 30, pp. 140,141.

[42]Don Matzat, *Christ Esteem* (Eugene, Oregon: Harvest House Publishers, 1990), p. 121.

[43]Heinrich Vogel, "The Old Testament Concept of the Soul," *Our Great Heritage*, Vol. 2, edited by Lyle W. Lange (Milwaukee: Northwestern Publishing House, 1991), pp. 214-217.

[44]Siegbert Becker, "Heaven and Hell," *Our Great Heritage*, Vol. 3, p. 666.

[45]Wilbert Gawrisch, "Eschatological Prophecies and Current Misinterpretations," *Wisconsin Lutheran Quarterly*, Vol. 84, No. 3 (Summer 1987), p. 202.

For Further Reading

Articles in *The Book of Concord: The Confessions of the Evangelical Lutheran Church*, translated and edited by Theodore G. Tappert (Philadelphia: Fortress Press, 1959):

Augsburg Confession and Apology: Article II, Original Sin; Article XVIII, Free Will; Article XIX, Cause of Sin.

Smalcald Articles: Part III, Article I, Sin.

Formula of Concord: Article I, Original Sin; Article II, Free Will.

Essays in *Our Great Heritage*, Vol. 2. Edited by Lyle W. Lange. Milwaukee: Northwestern Publishing House, 1991:

Dobberstein, Leroy. "The Doctrine of Offense."

Lillegard, George. "The Religions of the Heathen World." (An excellent essay on heathen religions as religions of works.)

Meyer, John P. "Original Sin" and "The Image of God, Genesis 1."

Raabe, John. "The Conscience."

Reim, Edmund. "Ancient Heresies in Modern Garb—Heresies Which Limit the Implications of the Fall of Man."

Vogel, Heinrich. "The Flacian Controversy on Original Sin" and "The Old Testament Concept of the Soul."

Das, Andrew A. *Baptized Into God's Family*. Milwaukee: Northwestern Publishing House, 1991. An excellent treatment of Baptism as God's answer to original sin in infants.

Scripture Index

Subject Index